# REROUTE

Wishing you love,
happiness, and prosperity.
— Geraldin Noemis
Diaz

# REROUTE:

## POST GRAD GUIDE TO SUCCESS — PHYSICALLY, MENTALLY AND FINANCIALLY

GERALDIN NOEMIS DIAZ

NEW DEGREE PRESS

COPYRIGHT © 2020 GERALDIN NOEMIS DIAZ

REROUTE:

*Post Grad Guide to Success — Physically, Mentally and Financially*

ISBN      978-1-63676-554-9  *Paperback*

          978-1-63676-130-5  *Kindle Ebook*

          978-1-63676-131-2  *Ebook*

# EPIGRAPH

———

*Twenty years from now you will be more disappointed by the things that you didn't do than by the ones you did do. So [. . .] sail away from the safe harbor. Explore. Dream. Discover.*

—MARK TWAIN

# DEDICATION

—

*To my mother and father, who believed in me when
I didn't believe in myself. I dedicate this book to you.*

You two brought me into this world and taught me the most
valuable lesson life has to offer—to be grateful for the little
things. Whenever I hit rock bottom, you were there. Whenever my bank account was close to $0, you were there. When
I couldn't walk because I messed my back up in the gym, you
were there to carry me and then push me around the hospital
in a wheelchair.

I have the best parents in the world.

You have devoted your lives to giving me the life you never
had growing up. You let me grow up with abundance in my
life. You two never made me feel like I lacked anything, even
if you were struggling to make ends meet. You have always
made me feel loved. You nurtured me to be the caring, giving,
and strong individual I am today.

I love you both and I hope your *reina* (queen) is making you proud each and every day.

With love, your one and only favorite daughter.

# CONTENTS

---

# INTRODUCTION:

# THE TRUTH

———

I had dreams after graduating from college. Enormous dreams, I'd say. I dreamed of becoming the first millionaire in my family. I thought I would be earning six figures just because I'm that awesome. Do you ever dream of becoming a big household name? Of having cool clothes, fancy watches, a nice car (my dream car is a Range Rover) and being a plant mom? (Yes, I said it, a *plant* mom). I aspired to achieve all these things too. I thought it was going to be easy.

Reality struck. Things turned into a bad episode of *My Super Sweet 16*. After graduation, I had no job lined up and no room of my own. I lived at home with my mother and brother in our two-bedroom apartment in downtown Brooklyn where I had grown up. Not sunny California where I thought I was going to end up. Not anywhere abroad where I hoped to travel.

I had no job, and prior to graduating, I didn't know how difficult it would be to get a job. Statistics show that the unemployment rate for recent college graduates has been steadily moving upward, currently at 3.9 percent.[1] For context, the natural state of unemployment is between 3.5 percent and 4.5 percent.[2] Not only are unemployment rates skyrocketing, but underemployment rates are also at an all-time high. The underemployment rate reflects the number of people accepting jobs below their academic or experience level. These individuals are stuck in gig economy roles, temporary work, or lower-end positions.

Being underemployed can be just as mentally and emotionally difficult as being unemployed. It impacts your energy and self-confidence and evokes fears about never having the future you imagined.

When I was unemployed, my days were unstructured. I mindlessly applied to places with no real goal but to simply get a job. I became desperate and torn. Part of me was ready to settle at any given moment for $15 an hour, and the other part reminded me to know my worth because I damn sure was not worth $15 an hour with my fresh college degree.

Or so I thought.

Despite knowing all this and having minimal work experience, I did have hope. This hope led me on a journey I wouldn't take back for anything in the world. I may have been drained in every sense but hope opened doors I didn't even know existed.

---

1    Darko Jacimovic, "College Graduates Unemployment Rate in the US."
2    Jack Kelly, "Recent College Graduates Have the Highest Unemployment Rate in Decades—Here's Why Universities Are to Blame."

Right after moving back to New York City, I made it my duty to rediscover myself outside of Geraldin the student and to become Geraldin the adult. The education system was all I had known my whole life. I had to find out now what my hobbies were and what foods I liked to eat since I had tastebuds now and didn't have to depend on ramen noodles, Domino's Pizza, and Monsters to keep me alive. I had to learn not to say, "Wine night, friends?" anymore because I no longer was living with friends, and my mom was not aware that I drank as much as I did. Most importantly, I had to prepare myself for the dreaded "Who are you?" question that would ultimately define my existence moving forward. I had to sit deep with that question, because outside of being a student, I couldn't truly answer who I was anymore.

By this point, you either think I am wild, or you completely relate to my story. I share with you my reality. Truth smacked me, but through it all, this was the best stage of my life. You will hear the majority of adults in their mid-twenties to late thirties say adulting sucks. My journey is just getting started, but I love it here. I am living the life I want. I am creating my reality and no one else is dictating it. For the past twenty-one years, other people dictated my life; these people were my parents. I went through elementary school, middle school, high school, and college because of them. I am grateful for the life they have given me, and it was time to take charge. I took charge by focusing on my well-being and my mental health and investigating my passions and my wants. After continuous digging (the work never stops), I've embarked on a journey of discovery.

Taking charge of your life looks like waking up and deciding how you want your day to go, prioritizing you, your mental health, your physical health, and your spiritual health. Often, even though we don't know it, we let society and those closest to us determine how our life is going to go. You need to distance yourself and spend some time alone tapping into your wishes and desires. No one knows you better than you know yourself. You spend twenty-four hours of the day, seven days a week with your thoughts—your mind.

*"How can I win in life if I ain't right within?"* I ask myself. You are allowed to create what you want; don't let anyone tell you otherwise. Once you realize what you want, you can develop a clearer vision of the direction you want to take. My advice to you is use the internet. We are blessed to live in a technological society. Use it to your advantage. Opportunities exist for anything you may be interested in, and if they don't, then you can create it. You create your own good fortune and opportunities.

Just because you don't know what you want to do for the rest of your life doesn't mean you're a failure. Beauty exists in not knowing; it gives you the bandwidth to be versatile and try different options to see what best suits you. Even if you end up not liking something, you still are able to get the experience and learn a lesson.

After graduating college, I went with my gut, following my instincts to discover what I wanted to do with my life, post-graduation. Deep down, you know what you want, but sometimes your environment clouds your judgment. Follow your gut and it will lead you in the right direction.

In this book, we will go on a journey, and I want you to maintain an open mind and be ready to take in all the good you're about to learn. This journey will challenge you and may push you past your comfort zone, but I promise you, if you take everything in, you will experience tremendous growth. I believe in you, and you should too.

You already picked up this book. That's step one and already speaks volumes to your willingness to take charge of your life and grow into who you want to be. After reading this book, you will have actionable steps and the courage to pursue the job of your dreams or start whatever endeavor you want. You will learn tips on networking, how to use LinkedIn to your advantage, and how reprogramming your thinking can help you much more in the long run. Let's get to it—financially, physically, and spiritually!

**CHAPTER 1:**

# GIVE YOURSELF A BREAK

First, I want you to pause. Thank yourself, celebrate yourself, and give yourself a big pat on the back. You've made it this far. You've graduated, whether it be from college, trade school, or cosmetology school. Whatever it may be, you did it. I am sure you doubted yourself countless times and wanted to give up, but here you are.

Disclaimer: If you didn't graduate, this book can still be beneficial to you because, ultimately, school isn't for everybody, and I get that. This book is for any individual who is starting in their career or unhappy in one.

You may be wondering—what is next? **This book will serve as a guide to ease your worries and help you turn the rejections in your life into opportunity, an opportunity to reroute.**

### UNHAPPINESS AT WORK

The typical life trajectory in the United States is to work a nine-to-five job until retirement at the age of sixty-five. Then at sixty-five, you're supposed to "enjoy your life," if you even make it to that age. This is what you have to look forward to after college. Doesn't that sound great? Yeah, no it doesn't.

Meanwhile, in the UK, according to research done by the Chartered Institute of Personnel and Development, 54 percent of workers have the option to operate outside of typical nine-to-five office hours.[3]

The CEO of Talent Management Consultancy at Guidant Global, Simon Blockley, stated:

> *Through offering the option to work flexibly, businesses can access a wider, deeper, and more diverse pool of talent to drive increased innovation, creativity, and profitability. Here at Guidant Global, 82 percent of our entire workforce have flexible working arrangements in place, allowing mums to fulfill their career goals, dads to spend more time with their children, neurodivergent people and people with physical disabilities the options to work in ways better aligned with their individual needs. We are also working with a number of clients to ensure that this approach to flexible working—and the associated benefits—are replicated across the wider business landscape.[4]*

Is this perhaps what the future of work looks like for the US? Maybe, maybe not. We as a society have some catching up to do.

---

3    Ann Swain, "Flexible Working Increase Five-Fold."
4    Ibid.

The majority of Americans are said to be "generally satisfied" with their jobs, but still, people frequently use phrases such as "Everybody hates Mondays" and "TGIF." The modern nine-to-five, eight-hour workday was invented by American labor unions in the 1800s and went mainstream thanks to Henry Ford in the 1920s. More than a hundred years later, workers are still prepared to accept the same shifts because we have become accustomed to it. It's the norm. As employees become increasingly frustrated with this traditional life path, they reimagine the systems.

Millennials are a driving force behind reimagining the future of work. Consider this. The 2016 Deloitte Millennial Survey found that two-thirds of millennials expected to quit their jobs by 2020, after only four years, citing both "dissatisfaction with work-life balance" and the "desire for flexibility" as two of the primary reasons.[5] Millennials want the flexibility to invest their time in other commitments and responsibilities. Most recent graduates agree that their pay is low, and they are overworked. That system explains why many debt payoff plans start at ten years after graduation.

PwC's "NextGen: A Global Generational Study" shared that millennials want to eliminate this outdated approach, stating that productivity should not be "measured by the number of hours worked at the office" but instead "by the output of the work performed."[6] Essentially, they want employers to pay them for the value they bring instead of the hours they put into work. When interviewing, this is what companies are

---

5    Ethan Schrieberg, "The 9-to-5 Workday Is So Last Century."
6    Robert Half, "Millennials: Workplace Rebels or Misunderstood Talents?"

looking for. What value will you add to the company? Value outweighs other factors.

## FEAR

The reason most people let fear control them is because they are scared. Fear of rejection is a direct result of seeing yourself as someone of low value and seeking the opinions of others to validate yourself.

I believe most individuals with low self-esteem blame their childhood experiences. I was afraid of rejection, because ever since I was a child, I had been called fat. (I am sure many of you could probably relate to the too-fat, too-skinny, never-just-right critiques.) I never spoke to guys first because I was never the friend getting "picked up," and this made me feel ugly and develop low self-esteem. Later on, this translated to my lack of boldness about my career options, because I never knew what to say to the adults asking. You might also not have a single clue about what you want to do in life. I never pushed myself out of this fear of rejection.

This fear then translates into our work space. We take low-ball offers and don't ask for more. Most of us may seem to be unhappy at work, but what keeps us there is fear and complacency. Fear of change, fear of failure, fear of it all. Ultimately, as explained in Robert Kiyosaki's *The Business of the 21st Century*, most individuals live in the *E* quadrant when it comes to cash flow. This stands for *employee*. We may aspire to earn more and live more luxurious lives, but ultimately what keeps us stuck in the *E* quadrant is fear. Fear to be different, fear to try something new, and most of all, fear of rejection.

Robert Kiyosaki breaks down business into four quadrants:

*The first quadrant are people who are largely dependent on their jobs for security. They devote the majority of their waking hours to that company and would be in serious financial trouble if that company were to fail or if they lost their job.*

*The second quadrant is for those who are self-employed, people who work for themselves. If the economy were to take a hit, the self-employed individual may have difficulty finding new projects or clients to work with. The self-employed have more time to devote to their own projects, however, they pay high taxes.*

*The third quadrant is business owners. Business owners are also self-employed, but they have taken their gifts and talents and transformed into experts in their specific fields. Essentially, they run their own shows. Business owners have control over everything—hiring and firing employees, establishing and improving production methods, and paying taxes. In this case, if the economy were to take a downturn, the business owner would have a plan on how to continue moving forward.*

*In the last quadrant are investors. This holds the highest level of financial security, according to Kiyosaki. Investors take what they earn and invest it into real estate, bonds, savings, and other assets that will multiply their initial input. Kiyosaki essentially presents a case that although most people are in quadrant one to feel secure in their jobs, jobs are not that secure, and there are other more fulfilling and richer ways to go about making money. The COVID-19 outbreak has been a clear indicator that job security does not exist, and, at any moment, you can lose it all.*[7]

Although it takes time to learn how to invest, get into real estate, or build a business, it is worth a try if you genuinely want to do it. We don't win anything living in fear. Take that leap of faith. If you want to be in that fourth quadrant, your best bet is to educate yourself—read books on finance, read blog posts, and watch videos. Do you want to be an employee your whole life? If not, do the work now. Let the fear go and invest in yourself.

Our lives revolve around what others think of us, and many of us end up living a life full of lies. Whenever my time comes, I never want to say, "I should've" or "I could've." We must live a limitless life, a fearless life.

Who controls your life? You? Then why are we still at that job, unhappy? Why are we scared to start a hobby? Why don't we have time to spend with our loved ones, and yet we are afraid to tell our boss? Fear is dictating our lives. Fear controls us.

Fear can be an empowerment tool. After graduating college, I let my fear empower and motivate me. Like many of you know, the job search after college is hard, but the knowledge you'll gain from this book will make it easier. I was receiving

---

7    Robert Kiyosaki and Kim Kiyosaki, *The Business of the 21st Century.*

hundreds of calls at all hours of the day and never knew which recruiter or which company was contacting me, so I created a job tracking sheet. I was embarrassed to pick up the phone and pretend I knew who it was when in reality, I had no clue.

Rejection after rejection I plugged in to my tracking sheet under the "offer" category. After writing *rejection* a minimum of thirty times, I decided to write *reroute*.

Why? My brain was processing the rejection as hurt. The rejection was fear telling me not to do something, to just quit. Rejection was personal, so I decided to write *reroute*, rewiring my brain to think about rejection as something more positive. Try this in your own job search and see how it makes you feel.

**THE PROCESS**

You may have been rejected once, twice, even over two hundred times like me, but once you think about it as rerouting, almost like a GPS changing gear after you miss an exit, you recognize that the destination is still the same. Even though the journey is a bit different.

With this in mind, every opportunity I missed allowed me to end at my ultimate goal, which was the creation of *Reroute: Succeeding Young* and my brand Grow with Gera. It almost made sense for me to get rejected so many times.

I may have done a technical sales boot camp, may have gotten various certifications, but I was lying to myself in every interview because I knew I didn't want to work a typical nine-to-five. I knew my life's purpose and journey was different than my peers. I wanted something more than just a job. I want to learn, grow, and invest in myself while investing in others. This is why on December 10, 2019, I decided I was going to write a book. The feeling of joy that came over me at this precise moment—in the shower listening to Oprah's *SuperSoul Conversations* podcast—was one I could've only dreamed of, but this was only the beginning.

### COLLEGE

Prior to that beautiful awakening moment, I had to write my book, I worked a nine-to-five job teaching high school students for two summers during my undergraduate years. I remember waking up at 6:00 a.m. to make it from downtown Brooklyn to the Bronx, the second to last stop on the four train, to be exact (New Yorkers know the struggle). I knew this couldn't be my life after graduating college. I was always tired, drained. All I did was work and come back home to sleep. The weekends came around, and I didn't have the energy to do anything.

At the time, I was just trying to make money to get by, and I didn't know these experiences would have such an impact on my future outlook at work, let alone on my future career path. For a little while as an undergrad, I wanted to be a teacher. I loved kids and always had aspirations of working with high schoolers. That goal soon changed, though, after teaching for two summers. As much as I loved helping children, I didn't want it to be my reality forever. Nonetheless, I learned so much from this experience and knew I would still impact high schoolers, just not through being a teacher. It took grit I didn't possess at the time.

During my senior year of college, I had a lot on my plate. I was president of my sorority and held six other positions, including vice president for my Greek council. I worked part time, was taking eighteen credits, and was doing an independent study. I've always been someone who does the most and tries to do it all on her own. This year was a huge eye-opener for me. I found myself crying a lot and drowning in work. I never asked for help because I was scared others would see me as weak. I had goals of going to graduate school to pursue social work, but after graduation, those plans changed. My heart wasn't in it to do what social workers do for what social work pays. It didn't make sense for me to get into that career because I knew I would ultimately end up unhappy.

Fear led me to not apply to these social work programs I had long been researching. However, this later turned into a blessing in disguise.

Life after college starts while you're still in it.

The sooner you start planning for your life afterward, the more manageable it will be. For me, it looked like planning a break from any coursework. By planning, I don't mean a set-in-stone plan, but you should have some structure for your upcoming goals.

If you want to take a break to focus on yourself, that's okay, too. However, you must have a goal with a deadline. Without a timeline, your goal is simply a dream with no destination. I wrote down my SMART (Specific, Measurable, Attainable, Realistic, Time-based) goals a few months after graduating in July. My goals started small. They encompassed all aspects of life because I knew I had a lot to improve on. I wanted to lose fifteen pounds by the end of August. I made it my duty to apply to at least fifty jobs each week. (This was before what I learned about how to get a job.) I also made it my duty to be more active and started working out and going on long walks throughout the summer.

SMART goals allow you to be realistic with yourself and hold yourself accountable. Writing down my goals allowed me to feel what I was working toward was more believable and achievable. I look at my goals every week to remind myself of what I want to achieve in the short term and long term. No matter how big or small the goal, write it down. When you get it done and cross it off, you will feel amazing and motivated to keep going.

**JOB HUNTING**

Getting a job wasn't as easy as it appeared. My aspirations of being a big household name were looking farther and farther away. I applied to over four hundred jobs in two months and received one curveball after the other. One day in July, I decided to apply to a technical sales boot camp my mentor had sent me. I had a little idea of what technical sales was. The program sounded cool and appealing, so I said, "Hey, why not give it a try?"

I had to start goal setting somehow, and this was my first step. I told myself this would be my big break to get to the six-figure mark I aspired to reach. First a six-figure salary, and then I would become a millionaire to solve the world's homelessness issue. *Cha-ching.*

After spending three months in class learning about technical sales, I did not want to pursue a fast-paced career in sales at that moment. Instead, I rerouted to applying to recruitment jobs.

I knew recruitment well and had the personality for it. Recruiting was similar to sales. Easy enough, right? *Wrong.* Rejections piled in yet again. I didn't even want to open my phone anymore because I knew the first notifications were going to be automated rejection emails.

"Thank you for taking the time to apply for this job. However, we have decided to go with another candidate. We wish you the best on your job search."

All the recruiters seemed to be copying and pasting each other's emails. At some point, I assumed these recruiters were racist, and I let that be the real reason behind my rejections. By this point, I thought to myself, *"Where the heck is this broken GPS rerouting me?"* Times got hard; my credit card debt piled up yet again, shortly after I paid it all off.

However, I didn't stop there after this massive defeat. I kept going. I like to think of myself as an Energizer Bunny that never runs out of energy. I had to pivot my interest because what I was doing was clearly not working. I decided to search for some help and paired up with agencies to see if they could help get me in front of the right recruiters. My experience was nice—I got to discuss potential interests—but it was short-lived because I soon recognized a pattern.

People in these agencies looked and sounded nothing like me. They couldn't cater to my needs. I was adamant. If I was going to work a nine-to-five, my vision and mission would have to align with the company I worked for. The companies they were working with truly had no interest in diversity and inclusion.

At this moment, I thought something was wrong with me. So, I tried my hand at digital marketing. I went through an interview and got to the second stage before deciding I was lying to myself. That was not where my interest lay. I could've stopped there, but instead, I decided to rewrite this narrative. I regained control of the person I was supposed to become. **In this case, it may seem like fear was stopping me, but my gut instinct told me to not go there. Although I typically avoided acting on gut instinct, this time, I decided to follow it.**

I had no job, no side gigs, no way to monetize my value even from my home. I shared my story and desperation for a job. I thought I was pretty pathetic, but little did I know, this transparency would open doors. This was my first try at really *asking* for something. A few weeks after my last rejection, I gave up completely on applications. I stopped searching for a job. Then I received a direct message from one of my sorority sisters. She asked if I was still looking for a job.

That was my first "big girl job," as most people would say, at a prestigious Kosher, upscale restaurant where the cost of a prime rib started at $500. Yup, you read that right. $500. *"Oh,"* I thought, *"They got* money *money here."*

**RESTAURANT JOB**

At this point, I was ready to take anything and everything that would pay. This was the point my narrative changed. All the rejections I had received led me to this moment. Funny enough, I didn't even do an interview to get this job. This is why expanding your network is key. In this restaurant, I was pushed out of my comfort zone, working long hours on my feet. Over eight-hour shifts just standing up, dealing with cranky customers and the privileged folk, and working in an extremely fast-paced environment.

Did someone say anxiety? I did get a few panic attacks while working there. The job was not fun at all, but it taught me a lesson: I can do anything I want in life.

I'd never had a job this demanding, but I was determined to learn from it. Working in a restaurant was not for me, but it did make me realize I had a great gift—connecting with people even in times of despair. On New Year's Eve 2019, we had over 200 guests flood into the restaurant, and we could only seat 160 at a time. Yes, I was one of the people working New Year's Eve. Poor entry-level people problems.

This one particular couple waited more than thirty minutes to be seated in a packed, loud, and busy restaurant. I could see the frustration in their faces and their body language, so what did I do?

I did what I knew best. Talk. We conversed about our backgrounds, our favorite foods, and where we went to school. Anyone might've thought we were longtime friends. Talking to people was second nature to me, as it's all I've known how to do since coming out of speech pathology therapy at the age of four because my mother feared I would never speak. Who knew her little girl would grow up into a talking machine?

In this precise moment, I learned why I was meant to be there. These stressful situations would better prepare me for my future life. I was meant to speak to those strangers because it would prepare me to be more comfortable speaking in front of large groups of people I didn't know. This experience also allowed me to have two of the best bosses a girl could ask for. I had to be vulnerable and communicative with them. My experience working at the restaurant was short-lived, since I quit one month after starting work there, but it helped me gain insight into what I did and did not want to do with my life.

### NETWORKING

Networking has been a huge asset that has allowed me to get all my previous jobs. Because of the connection I had with my counselor, I got my job working as a teacher for two summers in the Bronx. Throughout my college years, all the undergraduate assistant jobs I held were because of people I knew who recommended me to those jobs. After graduating, when I worked as the head of content for a sales organization for women of color, networking got me there. Lastly, having the right connections also got me the host job at the restaurant.

Whatever you want—any event you wish to attend or people you want to meet—go out there and do it. Don't let anyone stop you, and don't be scared to do things alone. Get out of your head and your comfort zone. **Having the right**

**connections can get you places.** I know it's intimidating to do this at first, but this is a part of pushing yourself to grow. Had I not posted that I was looking for a job, had I stayed stuck in my head, who knows if I would've gotten the opportunity to work at the restaurant and learn those important life lessons. Had I not been open to new opportunities, I probably would've avoided networking events and missed meeting some incredible people. I have gone to as many networking events as I possibly could throughout my time after college. I did this to get uncomfortable. I never knew how to pitch myself to people, how to tell them what I wanted in a few short sentences. I didn't even know what a pitch was.

Going to these events allowed me to speak to different people and learn to articulate what I wanted. I practiced selling myself with a great pitch. For those of you who may not know, a pitch is a thirty-second description of yourself. A good pitch should grab someone's attention and make people eager to get to know more about you, make them ask questions. A great pitch can get you through doors a résumé never could. Yes, you read that right.

A good pitch can get you through doors a résumé never could.

The reason all my plans came to fruition is because I set goals for myself.

My ultimate goal from attending these networking events was to get a job offer or meet people who could get me there. Along the way, I may not have received job offers, but I have met amazing individuals who have turned into mentors, life-long friends, and much more. Essentially, the universe had other plans for me, and sometimes that may be the case for you, and that is okay! Sometimes things don't work out, but they will always work out the way they are supposed to for the greater good. There is beauty in rejection.

As I attended these events, one door after another kept opening. The possibilities felt endless. If I wanted to refer someone to a company, I knew who to contact directly. I know people in almost every industry because I did the work to meet these people. Since I know a lot of people without a job, I felt I could be the crucial connection or the missing piece. I wanted to be the opportunity plug. The plug is an important role. So many people don't know the plethora of opportunities that exist out there and may complain, just like I used to. Whatever we want is out there, we just have to meet it halfway.

**CHAPTER TASK**

Research and write down ten companies you're interested in working for or collaborating with. Either DM them via LinkedIn or Instagram or contact the recruiter directly.

You may wonder, *"Why does she want us to do this?"* It will help you get out of your head and your comfort zone. Companies are looking for people like you—eager-to-learn, sponge like personality where you can easily learn and soak up what you learn and most of all people who can bring immense value to the table—so take your shot! Don't turn this page without first writing your list.

# CHAPTER 2:

# MENTAL HEALTH IS MENTAL WEALTH

───

For many of us, our mental health affects us unknowingly. It often operates under the radar. We don't always make it the priority it should be. I personally put my mental health on the back burner throughout my undergraduate years. After graduating, everything hit me like a truck, and not just any truck—an eighteen-wheeler.

We must recognize when we need help and ask for it. I know that can be easier said than done. I am grateful I was able to recognize when I needed help sooner rather than later. For many, especially those coming from families of color, therapy is looked down upon. It stems from a "we can conquer all with no help" attitude. Communities of color have endured generations of trauma and are expected to cope with it on their own. We have passed down this generational trauma like a mockery of a rite of passage. In truth, we are not allocated the necessary resources in our schools or within our communities to take care of our mental health.

Up-and-coming generations are learning to voice their opinions more and recognize when they need help. However, we still have a lot of work to do. Suicide is the tenth-leading cause of death across the United States population but is second among college students.[8] According to the National Alliance on Mental Illness, approximately one in five adults in the United States experience mental illness in a given year.[9] This fraction is not restricted to a certain race, creed, or color. In addition, according to the US Department of Health and Human Services Office of Minority Health, Black and African American adults are 20 percent more likely to report serious psychological distress than white adults.[10]

Despite this, African Americans are less likely than whites to seek treatment and more likely to end treatment prematurely. On one end, this is due in part to long-held beliefs related to stigma, openness, and seeking help, which can make African Americans and other people of color reluctant to reach out. On the other hand, professionals in the health care community must do the work to establish themselves as reliable and informative sources of support. You need to get to the root of your problems and face them to "live your best life," as the kids say. Everyone can benefit from therapy.

In the first few months after graduating, I thought I had conquered post-grad depression. In November 2019, I lost a

---

8   Eden David, "Rising Suicide Rates at College Campuses Prompt Concerns over Mental Health Care."

9   "Mental Health by the Numbers," NAMI: National Alliance on Mental Illness.

10  Victor Armstrong, "Stigma Regarding Mental Illness among People of Color."

close cousin and didn't properly mourn the loss. I was too focused on thinking, *"What would he want me to do?"*

My cousin would want me to be happy, so I chose to ignore the grief and to be happy. A few months later, I broke down in front of my father and brother because I'll never get my cousin back.

My brother told me, "I don't know how people are depressed and have all these issues. There's nothing to worry about." At that moment, I saw the issue with the way he thought. He was invalidating my feelings and his. This is the harsh reality of many Black and Latinx families. We negate conversations that have anything to do with feelings.

According to Mental Health America, 36 percent of Latinos with depression received care versus 60 percent of whites.[11] Bilingual patients are evaluated differently when evaluated in English versus Spanish, and Latinos are more frequently undertreated than are whites. Latinos are undertreated for a variety of reasons, but one of the main ones is that they avoid what is going on in the household and brush it under the rug. Furthermore, fewer Latinos go into the mental health field. Most health care workers may not speak Spanish or understand it, so how can they give a proper diagnosis with a language barrier? My parents and brother have never been through therapy. All the issues they have encountered in life they have endured with the "I can conquer all. Real mental

---

11  "Latinx/Hispanic Communities and Mental Health," Mental Health America.

issues don't exist" mentality. They never saw therapy as an option.

Fast forward to February 2020. I was in an uncomfortable situation that brought back memories of when I was sexually abused.

According to the Rape, Abuse, and Incest National Network (RAINN), the likelihood that a person suffers suicidal or depressive thoughts increases after sexual violence.

I was uncomfortable for months, scared to step outside. Something so normal now seemed like the hardest task to do. I was scared of seeing this man that put me in an uncomfortable situation. I was scared to be around men. I had no one to speak to in my household.

My day-to-day life was deeply affected. I knew I needed help. I woke up with stress and anxiety every single day. I lived in fear for my life. I cried every day and wondered if things would ever get back to how they used to be. Would I ever feel comfortable walking outside? Would I ever feel comfortable around a man again?

It had been years since I had talked about sexual assault. The first incident happened in my sophomore year of college, but this time, addressing the traumas I endured was unavoidable. My life took a turn for the worse when I was triggered in February 2020, and things went downhill fast. This moment made me realize all I had bottled up from the sexual assault had morphed into feeling like I was worthless and related to my depression, fear of the future, and, most of all, fear of life.

I went to therapy once a week and started using three apps in particular: Headspace, Shine, and Noom. The apps all helped me in different ways. They take an inside-out approach to therapy. Noom helped me rethink my relationship with food. The apps gave me a more psychological and habit-based approach to facing my depression. I liked it and know many who could benefit from this.

Any time I felt anxious or overwhelmed, I'd go to Shine or Headspace and listen to a meditation or write how my day is going and what has me anxious. This allowed me to get out of my own head and acknowledge my real thoughts. Noom allowed me to take care of my body and allowed me to reevaluate my food choices to make healthier decisions.

Sessions with my therapist allowed me to open up, which I wasn't used to doing. I never liked opening up; I was always the helper and never tried to make things about me and my problems. But after starting therapy, having someone listen to me felt nice, someone who would just listen and try to understand where I was coming from instead of putting me down. I learned to take deep breaths, which we as humans tend to forget. Being from New York, I never truly tapped into the power of my breath. Breathing techniques have allowed me to better cope with my anxiety and depression. Whenever you start feeling anxious, take deep breaths. Remove the distractions like phones and the TV. Focus on your breathing and let it ground you. At the end of the day, our breath is what keeps us alive. Cherish the small moments.

My life has completely done a 180-degree turn. Through my mental health practices, I now walk outside confidently again.

I no longer get sudden panic attacks. I can better control my anxiety through my breath. I focus on the present moment and not the traumas of my past. I adequately processed and moved on this time rather than burying it all. Putting your mental health on the back burner is almost like putting chicken in the freezer. (Sorry to the vegans and vegetarians out there.) You put the chicken in the freezer, and although you know you can keep it there for some time, at some point, you need to take it out. Dealing with your traumas is the same thing. You can avoid them for as long as you want, but eventually you are going to have to address them.

Therapy is crucial, as you cannot take on all the world's problems on your own. Talk it out, write it out, exercise it out—do what you need to do; because after graduation, real life starts knocking fast. I found it tough to explain therapy to my parents because of Latino and Black social norms. To my surprise, my therapy explanation was a smoother process than I thought it would be, and they were open to supporting me every step of the way. However, they kept questioning the real reason why I needed therapy. How could I explain the never-ending cycle of hopelessness, trauma, assault, depression, and anxiety? All in all, throughout my time in therapy, they always asked me how it went and genuinely expressed interest in seeing me get better.

After I was diagnosed in February 2020 with anxiety and depression, I realized I had been depressed since my junior year of college. At the time, I thought I had figured it all out on my own; in reality, I had just suppressed what I was feeling. This ideology came from what I was taught as a young girl—therapy was for the weak. I'd just figure it all out on my own, I thought, and things would be fine. Yeah, right. I had nothing figured out, and things weren't fine.

Since I lived with my mom during winter break of my junior year, I had to pretend to be okay. I kept thinking to myself, *"How would my mother react if she saw her daughter randomly burst out crying? How would she react if I didn't get out of bed all day? How would this affect her if she felt she failed as a mother?"*

I put her before myself, suppressing my feelings and shoving them into a little dark hole. That would come back full circle and affect me years later. Pushing my problems away didn't fix anything. Instead, it prolonged the healing process. Drinking didn't fix my problems either; it just numbed the pain temporarily. I was keeping busy with school, extracurricular activities, and partying. I was doing everything except focusing on the real issue at hand.

In February 2020, I chose to tackle my problems head on. I utilized not only therapy but also meditation, breathing exercises, music, journaling, and podcasts. This has been my form of healing, and it could be yours too. After living in a gloomy hole, I knew I never wanted to be that person again, so I made it my duty to discover things that would work for me and share my story with others.

**To change your life, first recognize you have a problem, and then be open to finding a solution.**

I know you can feel alone at times, like you have no reason to live, but things get better. Even in the dark, light will guide you, and I chose to follow the light. I share my story in the hope that it will inspire you to find a better place. I share my story to be the light in your cloudy storm. Whenever you feel alone or in need of reflection, reread this chapter.

Recognize when you are not feeling okay and know help is out there. Feel your mixed emotions. Accept that you may not know how to feel. Sometimes you just feel *bleh* and can't explain it. Slow down and breathe. Cry. Break down.

During my post-grad transition, I sometimes felt alone and like I had no one to talk to, but I always got myself out of those funks by focusing on my breathing and thinking about where I wanted to be in life. Take small steps. Think about the impact you can have on people's lives, the tremendous amount of goodness you deserve. Think about everything you have already overcome. Being present while still setting goals for my future reminded me why I needed to keep going.

When you're thrown off by the circumstances in your life, your body feels it, and you go into fight-or-flight mode. Your body can feel things before you can see them, before your mind acknowledges them. So, pay attention to your body.

Doing the things I've suggested above, or any other forms of healthy healing, will help you get back to your center and live a more prosperous life. **As humans, we tend to put others before ourselves. This time put you first.** You deserve it. You will win. You will live the life you desire.

**CHAPTER TASK**

For the next seven days, practice deep breathing. Allow it to ground you. You can do it for one minute, three minutes, five minutes, or however long you desire.

Deep breathing decreases stress, increases calm, relieves pain, stimulates the lymphatic system, improves immunity, improves energy, and helps support correct posture.[12]

Here's how you do it:

Inhale through your nose for three seconds, release through your mouth for three seconds. Close your eyes so you're not distracted by your surroundings.

Allow yourself to be in the present.

If you feel your thoughts drifting, come back to the present moment.

If you'd like, you can do this activity in silence or play relaxing sounds on YouTube, Spotify, Apple Music, Soundcloud, or whatever your preference.

Although this exercise may feel small and insignificant, long term, it has amazing benefits that can help you lead a more prosperous life.

---

12  Andrea Watkins, "Benefits of Deep Breathing."

# CHAPTER 3:

# FOCUS

———

**Always know your worth and what you bring to the table, especially during the job-seeking process.** Companies will undersell you if they see you as weak and vulnerable. This is how many employees end up unhappy and working long hours. Then they are afraid to negotiate and ask for a higher salary. To better equip you throughout your own job-seeking process, I will share tips on the following topics I wish I learned sooner.

- How your profile on LinkedIn should appear.
- How to directly contact people.
- Why you should go in with a clear purpose.
- How to approach interviews.

### LINKEDIN PROFILE PRESENTATION

Before starting your job search, know that LinkedIn is a free tool that should become your best friend. Companies and recruiters are active on LinkedIn. If you're trying to get your foot in the door, this is the way to do it. Before reaching out to potential employers and recruiters, make sure your LinkedIn profile is up and running. The last thing you want to do is contact someone and have them brush you off because of a simple mistake on your profile. Have someone look over your profile and tell you what you need to edit before reaching out.

I remember direct messaging so many individuals and getting rejected. Later on, my mentor told me I should have had a stronger headline and edited my bio to be more friendly to the eye.

### THINGS I DID WRONG IN MY BIO

- Long-winded and impersonal. My bio didn't explicitly say what I was bringing to the table. You have to articulate your value, so people want to connect with you.
- Not being specific. My headline stated I was a tech fellow at the company where I was doing my sales training. However, the lack of specificity allowed people to interpret this as anything. It also wasn't entirely who I was. I then changed my headline to:
  "Educating and empowering recent college graduates on how to use rejection as a tool for empowerment. 📇💡| Book Coming Winter 2020. 📖"
  Disclaimer: This was my headline before I started working a full-time job. I got creative with what I was doing instead of just writing "Actively seeking opportunities in XYZ." It was more about *showing* rather than telling people what I do. This allowed me to be more direct with who I engaged with and who engaged with me. You are so much more than just a job seeker. Let your personality shine through. If you're working on any side projects, mention that. My headline also allowed me to have specific key words in my description that would allow others to easily

find me. Key words like *educating, empowering, recent college graduates*, and *rejection* let others know what type of value I was bringing to the table.

- Having no call to action (CTA).

  Another crucial thing I learned during my sales training is to always have a call to action. A call to action prompts an immediate response or encourages a sale. When you can convey what you want clearly and effectively, you will get more done. Many companies may not have the bandwidth to post all the jobs they are hiring for, so the power of connection is key. Learn from my mistakes. A call to action should be in any emails you send, in the posts you put up, and in your headline. Doing this allows a recruiter to see your high level of engagement, which can prompt them to follow up with you if they have an opportunity available.

**DIRECT CONTACT**

"To stand out from the crowd," advised Mark Beal, the author of *Decoding Gen Z*, "work around the automated screening process that most large employers use these days." This advice by Beal can catapult you in your career. "Bypass the technology," Beal went on to say. "Leveraging connections will help you succeed."[13]

I spent endless hours applying through Indeed, LinkedIn Easy Apply, Glassdoor, Monster, and many other job search sites. Be careful with these platforms. When you submit your

---

13  Mark Beal, *Decoding Gen Z: 101 Lessons Generation Z Will Teach Corporate America*.

résumé through them, your résumé can lose its structure because of how the data tool processes documents. Recruiters get thousands of applications via mainstream application channels. Do you think they have the time to look through every single application?

The answer is no.

Did you know the majority of jobs are unlisted? Approximately 80 percent of open jobs are not posted online, yet the majority of people only apply online for jobs. In reality, networking and referrals fill 85 percent of all jobs

### WHAT IS A REFERRAL AND HOW DO YOU GET ONE?
A referral is when someone promotes the positive features of you or your business. An example of a referral is explaining to someone why a certain individual or business would be a good relationship for them to consider. **Only 1 of every 250 online applicants gets hired compared to 1 of every 4 referrals.**[14] Therefore, referrals are the most effective way to get hired.

**I suggest everyone get into the mindset of using referrals instead of applying for jobs directly online.** For the public market, the way most people apply to jobs, recruiters are only looking at key words. They don't see you as a person. Through the "hidden market," recruiters are able to focus on the whole person and look more into their past performance and their potential to succeed in the position. If you forget everything else I mentioned, remember this: Let referrals

---

14   Anthony Holloway, "My 21-Day Job Offer Story."

be your drive and motivation to change the avenues you're taking to find a job.

*You're twenty times more likely to get hired with a referral.*

An example of a referral from my personal life was when my mentor connected me to a woman who worked in sales. We had about two conversations and interacted with each other's content on LinkedIn. A few short months after connecting, I randomly met her in person at a networking event, and she was one of the panelists. That gave me a perfect segue to meet other panelists too, since she was connected to them and I was connected to her. We had a conversation and bounced off each other well.

Fast forward a couple of months, I interviewed for her employer but didn't end up getting the job.

I didn't prepare well enough. I didn't do sufficient research. Research is key in job interviews. Little did I know that her company was merging with a second company to create a new and revamped company.

A few weeks after this interview, I posted on LinkedIn I was looking for a job, and she commented with a request to email her. I did, and she connected me straightaway to a recruiter. I hopped on a call and set up interviews within a matter of days.

I landed a job I love within three weeks of the first call. Who knew *job* and *love* could be in the same sentence? Especially for someone like me who didn't want to do the whole nine-to-five. Funny how life works. Had I not had this connection, who knows where I would've ended up.

If you want to get a job, your best bet is to directly contact someone inside your target company. Connect with them on LinkedIn or reach out to them on social media. Talk to them as you would an acquaintance; be formal but let them know you have done a bit of research about them professionally and would like to learn more.

**APPROPRIATE MESSAGE EXAMPLE**

"Hello [insert name here], I see you have interests in [insert interests here]. I wanted to speak to you about this because I am interested in diving into this sector and would like further advice on how to navigate this. I am available at [insert calendar link or two potential dates and times]; I would love to hop on a call with you at your earliest convenience."

In this example, you are making a clear call to action and getting straight to the point. Short, sweet, and direct.

Ideally, you want to build rapport with the person. Direct message them and establish a strong relationship. People, especially recruiters and CEOs, do not have a lot of time, but if you are honest and direct, they are more likely to respond than if you fluff up the reason you are reaching out. If they don't follow up with you, it's not the end of the world. Don't think of it as a rejection. After all, they are usually busy people. They could even follow up with you later, even if that means months later. I've had people respond to me two months after I sent a message. Go in with the mindset of "if it is meant to be, it will be." **Whatever is meant for you will not miss you.**

Aim to contact fifty to one hundred contacts per week, roughly ten to fifteen people per day, to start. This way you give yourself more opportunity and could potentially end up with more offers, giving you options. Not everyone will respond, but the more people you reach out to, the more doors will open. Closed mouths do not get fed, so advocate for yourself and what you want, and again, be intentional and direct.

**KNOW WHAT YOU WANT**

To stand out, you need to be different. Take a different approach, like writing a creative cover letter or direct messaging your favorite influencer. Be different—you weren't born to blend in. You were born to stand out! Use and maximize your gifts and assets.

When you reach out to anyone, be intentional and say what you want to say with your chest. When you are clear on what you want, the *how* starts to show up. If you are seeking to add value, people will not deny that. Hiring managers and peers connect and resonate with people who are bringing value into their lives.

Define your mission. Where are you going?

What do you want your life trajectory to be?

If you're not clear with what you want, take a skills test. I didn't know what I wanted, and I took a skills test because I felt lost. Skills tests allow you to see where your strengths and weaknesses lie and what potential career paths you can take.

**When you're open to anything, you're open to nothing.** This is the cold, hard truth. I learned this while interviewing.

The interviewer would ask, "What are you interested in?"

I'd say, "Well, I am interested in everything. I like sales, tech, digital marketing, and recruiting."

Instead I sounded desperate, I was all over the place like I didn't know what I wanted. I thought I looked like I had expertise in all these fields despite not having a lot of experience.

When I focused on what I was really interested in and stopped lying to myself and letting my circumstances define my interests, I was better able to navigate the job market and, essentially, my life. My "dream job" was working somewhere where I could do something I enjoyed while still having time for educating recent graduates on how to better navigate post-grad life. Through my rejections, I redirected myself to where I am now. I have a job surrounded by people who genuinely care about my success. I write. I create content, and, most of all, I empower and educate those around me through sharing my story.

I now feel more suited and ready to speak to individuals as a coach and a mentor. My life's purpose is to empower and elevate others, either through the content I create or by having a chat with someone at work. If you don't know your *why* and what you want to do right away, don't worry. You will find it just like I did. It may take a few days, months, or even years, but you can get your feet wet to figure out what suits you. Had I not worked in a restaurant, I probably wouldn't have known how much I disliked the restaurant industry. Had I not worked with high schoolers, I probably wouldn't have known how hard teaching is.

All in all, this is why you should **get clear on what you want**, so you can better articulate yourself. Although I always went to networking events, I found it hard to explain what I did. Other people would always ask, "What do you do?" and I never knew how to answer. Now I realize it is ok to say you're figuring things out. Even if you feel a little lost, ask people what their jobs are and what they like about them. Maybe you'll come across something you like through speaking with individuals. You don't have to do just one thing or the other; if you want to work in sales and be a volleyball coach on the side, do that, but find one thing you like first and go from there. An abundance of jobs and opportunities exist out there, some we've never even heard of. Maybe that could be your next big thing. I believe in you!

### RÉSUMÉ AND INTERVIEW

Before you go out and look for connections and specific jobs, get right with your résumé. I've had some pretty rough résumés, I'd say, but through my experience over the past few years, I learned about the value a résumé can hold. When you contact recruiters directly, they will likely ask for your résumé.

Your résumé should be one page and should have no more than two to four bullet points explaining each position you have held or currently hold. Depending on the jobs you're applying to, one key pointer is to tailor your résumé to that industry.

For example, if I am applying to sales development representative positions, I will highlight my sales experience at the top, since most people's eyes are drawn there. Use descriptive words and hard numbers. People like seeing numbers on résumés because numbers are measurable and can speak to your success.

If you hosted events while in school with your club, perhaps think about writing "hosted five events each quarter" followed by the purpose of these events. The better you articulate the value you have brought, the easier your job search will be.

The approach you take to get to the job should be how recruiters recruit. Be prompt with your responses. Speak to recruiters directly, or if you can't get a hold of them, contact a second or third connection via LinkedIn. Establishing a solid relationship foundation is key during this stage. When you put yourself in a position to give, to add value, you get a lot more return on your investment.

Connecting with recruiters will help your job search process go smoother because recruiters are always posting what's going on in the market and can be your direct ticket to a referral.

**When interviewing, make it about the company.**

For example, if you know someone has just interviewed the founder or CEO of the company for a podcast, mention that. If they just received funding, congratulate them. Do your research, and it will speak volumes about your character. Most people go into interviews and think about *me, me, me* and forget why they are there. Don't let that be you. Go into it with a *we* mentality because you will be working alongside others.

**Something I learned throughout the interview process is to be overprepared.**

Any time I had an interview, I used a huge spiral notebook to take notes on every important company fact and to make personal connections. I recorded what resonated with me about the company and information on the interviewer.

One of my favorite questions to ask interviewers is "What's your favorite and least favorite part about your job?" This always for some reason takes them aback because they are never used to getting asked personal questions.

"Thank you for asking," they would often reply after they answered. "No one has ever asked me that."

People like nice people. You know the phrase *kill them with kindness*? It goes with everything in life, because people can be mad at you, but they can't be mad at you for being nice.

Have a list of questions ready to ask for all your interviews. I suggest preparing three to five questions based on what you want to know. Some example questions are:

- What are the top three priorities for this company in the coming year?
- Why did you choose this job?
- What do you believe this company offers that is different from most other companies?

These questions can signal your interest in the company or the person and are also not too serious. They lead you to build rapport with the interviewer.

### QUESTIONS YOU MAY BE ASKED

1. What are your biggest strengths? What are your biggest weaknesses?
2. Why do you want to work here?
3. What compensation do you expect?

I typically like to turn this question around on them, so I don't leave all my cards on the table. I ask, "How much does a person with my type of experience typically get compensated?"

If they turn it back around on me again, I always have market research to back up why I should get paid a particular amount.

4. Why are you the best person for this position?
5. What is your ideal work environment?

6. What are your short-term and long-term goals, and how does this position fit into that?

Here, whatever you do, do not mention anything that could indicate to employers that you plan on leaving soon.

7. How do you work with other people?
8. Tell me about what you would do during your first thirty days in this role.
9. Tell us about a time you had a problem and what you did.

Interviewers can ask a wide array of questions, but these are some that typically come up. Have answers prepared, have someone practice with you before an interview or record yourself, or even just speak out loud. Preparation is essential.

**TRANSFERRABLE SKILLS**

Wherever you choose to go in life make sure to develop transferable skills. Transferrable skills are skills that you can use in any field you go into for example active listening, problem solving, critical thinking. My suggestion of trans-ferrable skills you should work on developing are as follows: decision-making–because decisions will always have to be made, and you don't want to be deemed indecisive. Hav-ing good decision-making skills will allow you to lead with confidence. Collaboration–if you can't work in a team or with other people you will not be successful in life. Com-munication–communication is a skill everyone, regardless if you're behind a computer all day or in front of people all day, should possess. Because the better you are able to articulate yourself, the fewer problems you will have. Empathy–this is a skill many individuals lack, but it is so important to possess.

When you lead with empathy, you will be seen as a trusted advisor, thus more people will believe and trust you. Always ask yourself, *Wherever I end up how can I take my skills with me and apply them accordingly?*

**Persistence will get you through doors failure can't.** If you quit any time things get rough—for example, after bombing your first interview or not getting the job you desired—you will end up right back where you started and be more upset that you gave up.

In addition, just because you got denied once doesn't mean it will happen again as I illustrated with the story I shared earlier in this chapter.

Companies ask themselves, "Do I like you?" You will have to work with other team members. They ask, "What can you do for me now?" Companies want to keep growing and generating revenue, so can you hop on board and keep up? Lastly, they ask, "What can you do for me in the future?" Are you thinking about their position as a long-term gig, or are you going to quit the moment a better opportunity comes along? Put yourself in their shoes.

**Building relationships is crucial no matter what you do.** People like people who resemble them. **Be authentic, because authenticity is rare nowadays, and you possess that gift free of charge.** I know you may feel scared to directly contact someone, but if you don't do it, somebody else will. **Be the exception, not the rule.**

**CHAPTER TASK**

Contact seventy people directly through LinkedIn this week. Disperse them throughout the week, ten or so each day, or do them all in one day. Be intentional. Be direct. Build your network and get out of your comfort zone. Do this so you can see the power of networking and establishing relationships. You've got this!

## CHAPTER 4:

# LIFE PASSION AND FINANCE

———

Many of us go our whole lives not knowing our passion. We never sit down with ourselves and figure out what lights a fire within us.

Luckily, for me, from a young age, I knew I was meant to be a helper. I wasn't exactly sure what I would do with this, but I knew I loved helping people in whatever way I could. Throughout my whole college experience, I aspired to get my master's in social work after completing my undergrad. I told everyone that was my plan. My father told so many people that his little girl was going to get her master's. I even went to several open houses for schools and started the application for a few social work master's programs. I was so ecstatic about the possibility of being the first person in my family to get my master's.

Then one day something told me *now is not your time*. Ever since, I never looked back. Any time something isn't right a little voice arises in my head and tells me not do something. This was my gut instinct. It made sense because my undergraduate career was an exhausting one. So exhausting, I even had to withdraw for one semester because my mental health was on the line.

Throughout my journey, I knew I wanted to help people, but I wasn't prepared to go through any more schooling or acquire any more student loans. So, I had to dig deeper and start asking myself questions like:

- Who did I want to help?
- How could I help them?
- What is my gift?
- What is different about me?
- What is my story?
- What are the problems these people are facing?
- What are their desires, wants, and needs?

Although I was unsure about where I was headed, I shared my story via my social media networks. I also started my own blog, a website, and a brand called Grow with Gera, which has become my staple. Through all these platforms, I share my story. I am good at sharing experiences with other people. Grow with Gera is my post-grad life journal. Through the trials and tribulations, I realized my passion was to help recent graduates and those unhappy in their current jobs live more fulfilled lives.

I went through a series of courses, boot camps, and much more to get to where I am. My job throughout this journey has essentially been to collect the information and put into words what we all should've grown up learning. As a first-generation college grad, I didn't know the tips and tricks of how to apply for jobs. I didn't know how to pay off my loans or where to look to find loan information like forbearance and deferment options. I had no clue how to go about purchasing a house. I had no clue about how to handle finances or even how to balance a checkbook. These are all things I had to go out of my way to learn.

My parents didn't know; therefore, I didn't either. As a first-generation college grad, especially if you're from a Latinx, Black, Brown, or Asian background, you're assumed to have three job options: a doctor, a lawyer, or a teacher. Most of us may head down these paths to make our parents proud and because we believe we'll make tons of money in these fields.

Then we quickly realize we don't like that career path. Colleges promote participating in clubs and organizations, for you to find out what you like. Don't go by what your parents told you to like. I had to go out, do the work, and put myself out there, but I loved every step of the way. Because I acquired so much knowledge, I can now use it to help transform lives.

Upon graduation, I immediately created a plan for myself to get rid of my student loans ASAP. I graduated with just a little over $40,000 in loans, and that was for one undergraduate degree. Imagine a master's degree with no financial support. According to the Federal Reserve, the average college debt among student loan borrowers in America in 2016 was $32,731. This is an increase of approximately 20 percent from 2015 to 2016. Most borrowers have between $25,000 and $50,000 in student loan debt. People that graduated with their undergraduate degree over ten years ago are still paying back loans.

My aspiration was to be debt free sooner, but the debt repayment strategies loan servicers implement all start at about a ten-year repayment and more, incurring interest over the course of those years, so you pay more. Personally, I am a strong advocate of paying your loans off as soon as possible and figuring out whether consolidation is best for you financially. Do whatever is best. If it means to refinance or put the loans in forbearance, so be it. Everyone has their own individual strategy that will work best for their circumstance, so do your research.

Here are nine terms you should know when it comes to student loans:

*Exit Counseling:* When you are graduating or attending school less than half-time, you'll need to do exit counseling.

*Consolidation:* With consolidation, you combine your loans into one monthly payment with one servicer. Consolidating your loans may make it easier to keep track of all your loans if you have more than one student loan with more than one servicer.

*Annual Percentage Rate (APR):* This percentage is the interest rate you will pay on your loan over time.

*Deferment:* This is a set period of time during which the repayment of your student loans is delayed. A variety of different types of deferments exist, including in-school, unemployment, economic hardship, or active duty military service deferment. You will often need to complete a deferment application through your lender and provide proof and documentation of your eligibility.

**Forgiveness:** Depending on the type of loan, you may qualify for partial loan forgiveness. This means that those loans get "erased," and you no longer owe that portion of the loan.

**Forbearance:** Depending on the type of loan you have and your lender, you can qualify for forbearance if you are having trouble making your payments. Forbearance allows you to stop making payments for twelve months while interest continues to accrue.

**Grace Period:** Most lenders offer a grace period, a certain length of time after you graduate or stop attending college full-time when you do not yet have to make payments on your student loans.

**Gross Annual Income:** Your gross annual income is the income you earn in one year before taxes. This number will be used when filling out the FAFSA, applying for loans, and to determine your repayment plan once you are paying back your student loans.

**Interest Rate:** You must pay interest to your lender in exchange for borrowing money. A fixed interest rate will not go up or down during the term of the loan, whereas variable interest rates can shift depending on financial markets.[15]

---

15   Kristen Kuchar, "Student Loans 101: Vocabulary."

As someone who had no means of income and no guidance on how to do anything from paying off loans to applying for jobs, I decided to go out and explore different networking events to find out what opportunities existed. Going to networking events not only allowed me to open the doors for a chance at a job but also educated me about the value of the dollar and how to handle my finances. At this moment I became the captain of my ship and took a hold of my future.

Everyone has a story to tell. Be the narrator of your story. Everyone has something to offer. I am sure you have gifts and talents you are sitting on that could be making you bank right now but you are perhaps afraid to put yourself out there. Never feel worthless or as if you have nothing to bring to the table, because **everyone has a gift to contribute. Your best you is a superhero, and your worst you has room to grow.**

Everyone's passion is different. Some find it sooner in life and some find it later. Trust that everything you're going through serves a purpose. All the hardships, the redirections, the good moments, and the scary moments. They are what makes your beautiful existence.

Sit down and ask yourself the following:

- What are three things I love to do?
- What are three things I hate to do?
- What are my top three money goals for the next six months?
- What is holding me back from being where I want to be financially?
- Lastly, what are three things I would do regardless of pay?

Once I sat down and answered these questions, it all clicked. Three things I love to do is share and spread knowledge, talk, and listen. Three things I hate to do are be around negative people, hang around people with a closed mindset, and be overlooked or go unacknowledged.

My top three money goals are becoming debt free, moving out and living below my means, and increasing my savings by at least 5 percent every month.

My student loans are holding me back from where I want to be financially.

Three things I would do regardless of payment would be to (1) share my story and empower those around me, (2) continue to sing like no one is watching because it brings me joy, and (3) crack jokes because comedy is a language we can all communicate through despite race, religion, or gender.

When answering these questions, be authentically vulnerable, as it'll allow you to discover your truth.

Sometimes you'll even need someone else to read what you have said because it's hard to figure it all out on your own. I decided to get a financial advisor because finance isn't an expertise of mine. This has helped me not only better handle my finances but also helped me achieve my goals more quickly without feeling stressed about money.

Life coaches and consultants are also good resources if you have the means to afford one. I chose to pass my ideas by wise people who are in higher positions than I am to truly get a valuable opinion. Speaking to the right people can pivot you in the right direction.

Let this guide you to uncovering your passion and lead you to becoming your best financially thriving self. It may take some time to find your passion, but once you find it, let it drive you to do whatever you want. If you want to climb Mount Everest, prepare for the climb. If you want to pay off your student loans in a year, do it. Write your plan out. If you want to buy a house in three years, get to it. If you want to get to a senior position at a Fortune 500 company or at a startup, work toward it. Create a plan for yourself. Whatever you want, you can achieve, but figure out your *why*, your passion, and let that lead you. Let that fire ignite even when the road appears dark. In those moments of hardship, you will realize your true potential.

I had to sit through uncomfortable therapy sessions and depression and panic attacks to find out what I really wanted to do. The journey was rough, but it led to a beautiful creation. Everything in your life has meaning if you choose to give it meaning. Life isn't about discovering yourself but rather about creating yourself. You create and reinvent yourself every day. You add a new piece to the puzzle every day.

**CHAPTER TASK**
I want you to do some deep soul searching.

- What fuels your fire?
- What are your top three overall life goals?
- What are your top three finance goals?

Take twenty minutes to write what you like on one side of a piece of paper and what you don't like on the other side. Put on some theta wave sounds while you're at it to stimulate your subconscious. Truly home in on what fuels and motivates you and go from there. You've got this. Don't overthink it! Let it flow out of you naturally.

# CHAPTER 5:

# LET'S TALK HUSTLES!

———

Let's go deeper into finances! Many people may tell you money doesn't equal happiness, but when you get aligned mentally, spiritually, and physically, money will add to that happiness. Money tends to be a roadblock preventing many of us from getting where we want to be. If you come from a background like mine—growing up in a poor Caribbean household, living in the projects, using food stamps to pay for groceries—you most likely don't have a clue about finances. Just because no one educated your parents about how to create multiple streams of income or how to save doesn't mean you have to continue the poverty cycle. From the moment I graduated, I set out on a path to break the cycle and give my parents the life they gave me. They faced many hardships but always did their best to get me what I needed. Even with the little money they made they never made it feel like we lacked anything.

Background story about me and money. My dad and mom created a savings account while I was in high school to give me when I later went off to college. I decided not to touch the money until after I graduated college.

I thought the money had accumulated great value after more than eight years in the savings account. I was completely wrong. My parents opened my savings account in a brick-and-mortar bank with an interest rate of about 0.01 percent. In plain English, this means it didn't accumulate even a dollar during the eight years I left it alone. A piece of me wanted to be mad at my parents, but I couldn't; their lack of finance and investment education wasn't their fault.

I later sat down with my mother and told her, "Let's move the money to a high-yield savings account." A high-yield savings account typically pays twenty to twenty-five times the national average of a standard savings account. For example, if I put $1,000 into a high-yield savings account with a rate of 1 percent for a year, it will become $1,010. Even without adding additional savings to the account every month, this is still the case. Therefore, my mother and I decided to move my money to a CD, which stands for certificate of deposit. At the time, this seemed more appropriate. Certificates of deposit are a secure form of time deposit, where money must stay in the bank for a certain period of time to earn a promised return. We let $10,000 sit in the CD for five months, and it accumulated seventy-five dollars. That might not seem like a lot, but when my parents' previous efforts had accumulated less than a dollar over the course of eight years, it made me very happy.

Finance isn't something you learn in elementary, middle, or even high school, let alone college, unless you take a class on it, which often is only open to people in a finance major. The majority of first-generation Latinx, Black, and Brown students go their whole lives not knowing about the different types of retirement funds, matching options at their companies, or anything else pertaining to finances. We have to educate ourselves and then educate our parents. So many of us continue to live in an endless poverty cycle because we don't know any better. We aren't educated on how to make and save money. We don't know how to invest or trade stocks.

Instead, we know about falling into overdraft and spending excessive amounts of money on things we don't need. I know many individuals who constantly overdrew their bank accounts during and after college. Don't let this be you. They'd overdraw because of clothes shopping, eating out, spending nights at bars, and much more. Most of us simply spent recklessly. We were young and didn't have a care in the world. We were just trying to make the most of our college experience, thinking we'd worry about real life later. Banks rack up large sums of money in overdraft fees from overdrawn accounts. The bank is ripping you off, keeping the disadvantaged poor, and propelling the endless cycle of poverty. If you are running low on funds, check your bank statements for overdraft fees. The last thing you want to do is be in debt and then get hit with overdraft fees.

According to the 2019 Money Matters on Campus survey conducted by AIG Retirement Services, only seventeen out of the fifty states require a personal finance course as a mandate for high school graduation, and only seven of those require testing of those skills for graduation.[16] Additionally, only 35 percent of college students have taken a personal finance

---

16    Sarah Wood, "New Survey Finds College Students Lack Financial Literacy."

course in high school. Just like all other mandatory courses such as math, history, and English, financial literacy should be a mandated school subject taught from kindergarten through high school and into college.

College students don't know how to handle money because we are not taught how; this is why a lot of us live eating terrible foods and purchasing unnecessary things. After college, money only gets tighter. From the moment I graduated, I knew I had to get creative with my approaches to making money. Debts pile up—credit cards, student loans, car payments (if you have one)—and bills like Wi-Fi, phones, and subscriptions don't stop.

Times may be hard, but I want you to flourish. The way I see it, we've all worked really hard and shouldn't have to be stressed if we decide to spend some money. If you want to go out to that happy hour or treat yourself after a hard week at work, you shouldn't feel like you're overly restricting yourself with your expenses, but you also need to find a balance between necessities and wants. Once you find that balance, you will be able to adequately save and still be fulfilled.

The only way we are taught to make money is through a job. Let me tell you the truth. The way things are going, if you're only planning to work a job and have no financial literacy, things are not going to go well. Nowadays, you need multiple streams of income to live unless you own your own business where you can make unlimited amounts of money. Luckily, in this chapter, I will share ways to make money outside of a job.

We live in a technological society where a multitude of ways exist to make money outside of a traditional job. I've never been able to wrap my head around equating your time to money. This is truly what initiated my search for more ways to make money because I wanted to be in charge of how much I made based on the value I brought and not a dollar amount per hour. Typically, the more hours you work, the more money you make, but then you end up working yourself to death and hating your job if you don't find a balance. We need to use this global technology to our advantage. All the ways to make money in this chapter are doable; all you have to do is start with one.

Right after graduation, one of my favorite pastimes was to search "ways to make money from home." My internet browser history looked like endless articles on how to make money from home "easy money," side gigs, you name it, I was searching for it.

**SOME PROVEN TACTICS TO MAKE MONEY**

1. **Online user testing.** You can get paid for reviewing a product or service. Search sites or find people on social media that would pay you to use their product or service in exchange for a review.
   a. I have used this tactic before. I bought a product (an eyelash growth serum) and was asked to give an honest review in exchange for a product or gift card. After submitting my review, I was given a $15 gift card. Although this isn't a huge sum of money, it helped me bring down the amount of a future purchase I made.

2. **Sell your photos and videos.** I know many of you may have sunset pictures or cool graphics on your phone. You can sell them, and people will buy them from you.
3. **Negotiating referrals.** If you are well connected or don't mind reaching out to people, this may be a cool opportunity for you. Some companies give out bonuses for people who get the most referrals. All you have to do is ask, come to an agreement with the person or company, and get to work.
4. **Freelancing.** Sell a service or product on your terms and time, and you can charge however much you wish. Many sites hire online tutors. Get paid for any skill you have to offer—graphics, translation, or even transcription services. Websites such as Upwork and Fiverr are some of the most popular gig economy sector sites.
   a. I had experience with one that paid between twenty and twenty-five dollars an hour to teach kids English. Again, all you have to do is use Google. The same way LinkedIn became your best friend for your job search, let Google become your best friend for your research. If you are looking to gain experience before freelancing, look into micro freelancing or click working where you get paid for completing small tasks.
5. **Guest lecturing.** Universities and colleges often are looking for guest lecturers, and the topics are endless. This not only allows you to generate money for yourself but also gain exposure and build an audience.
6. **Course creation.** If you can identify a pain point (problem) in a specific demographic, you can create a course to add value to someone's life and profit from it.
   a. Large sums of money can be made here. If you don't feel like enough of an "expert" to create an online

course, find people who are and interview them and create research and content based around your findings. And of course, always give proper credit. Online courses are one of my favorite ways to generate income too, because you put it out one time, and it does the work for you. If you need inspiration, go on Udemy. They have tons of online courses on a variety of topics.

7. **Affiliate deals.** Refer people to a business and get a certain percentage of the generated revenue. You make a certain percentage of profit based on the amount of business you bring in.

8. **Sell research.** If you are into research, you can sell it.

    a. Data has power. This is your secret weapon in business that allows you to know your competitors. In business, you always want to be better than your competitors. If you enjoy doing research, ask a small business if they would pay you to research their competitors to help them better leverage how they sell and market their products.

9. **Bartering for a percentage of sales.** If you are good at selling or negotiating prices and you know someone who is struggling to sell, for example, their coaching program, help them bring in clients for a particular fee. Again, this allows you to build relationships and generate revenue. In this example, you make money by helping sell someone's product almost as if it were yours.

10. **Content writing.** You remember writing those long essays and finals, right? Well, you can get paid for that skill. People always need content writers for their books and blog posts. You can write these posts for them or edit them if you have an eye for this.

11. **E-book creation.** This is similar to creating a course, because you're again adding value to someone's life, but the e-book may be less complicated to create. Your e-book can be about anything you're interested in, as long as you see its ability to fix a problem.

   a. For example, people are always going to be health conscious, so maybe you can write an e-book on how to lose or gain weight.

12. **Recording audio.** If you're not much of a writer, this is a cool way to generate income that allows you to try something new. You can sign up online and record voice overs and make money from this.

13. **Monetize your blog or YouTube channel.** Use ads or sponsors to earn money through the subscribers you have.

   a. If you are consistently putting out material, people will have no problem supporting you if you decide to sell something because you've already established trust. This trust will make it easier for you to sell and will attract a larger audience.

### SOME OF MY METHODS

1. I've done online user testing a few times before. Oftentimes, I buy the product and only have to write a review for it, and I get reimbursed for what I spent on the product and/or a gift card to spend on anything I'd like.

2. I've also done freelancing. While freelancing, I created graphics and catchy captions for a specific organization. This allowed me to explore my creativity and use my time to make some money, even just enough to pay my phone bill and save the rest.

3. I've dabbled in monetizing my blog and YouTube channel but didn't have enough time to devote to it. If you, like

me, enjoy writing or being in front of the camera sharing what you know, try it. You can learn so much from doing this. Even though people have said being a blogger or a content creator is not a "real job," if you have any experience in this sector, you know the amount of time and energy it requires. It's rewarding, and you're able to run on your own time.

4. Lastly, course creation is something I am working on because I like the idea of putting out a product one time and getting unlimited sales from it. There are so many free and paid resources online to help you launch a course too, and it can be about anything ranging from how to make candy apples all the way to how to monetize your blog. The possibilities are out there for you to have an abundance of money.

All of the above methods reinforce the ideology that community building is key. **Your network is your net worth.** Even if you can't get a job, you can do business with someone through one of these methods, and this can pay off in the future. If you write or edit a piece for someone and later down the line one of their colleagues is writing a book, they could recommend you. Always keep doors open. You never know what one relationship could blossom into.

**CHAPTER TASK**

1. Open a high-yield savings account if you don't already have one. You don't have to start with a large sum of money. If you want to be ambitious with the amount you put into this account each month, you can. If not, be more conservative. Whatever you do, set up a plan and stick to it. Set yourself up for financial freedom, not financial

doom. Think about all the food you buy or clothes you buy only not to eat it or wear them. Save, save, save. You've got it! Let's get this money!

2. If you are having a hard time finding a job or struggling to make ends meet, dive into a side hustle. Whatever you want, just try it. If you make five dollars, you could make thousands more. You just need to try. Don't sit on the skills and talents you were born with.

## CHAPTER 6:

# MY BEGINNINGS WITH FINANCIAL FREEDOM

———

Now that we have multiple ways to make money, let's create an actionable plan. If you have debt to pay off, start small. For me coming out of college, I had no idea how to build my credit (make those payments on time!) or how I would pay off debt. I wrote in my journal, "I will pay off my student loans within the next two years."

I let go of the *how* and did what I knew best, controlling my spending. Instead of impulse buying, I asked myself, is this a necessity? It took a lot of willpower in the beginning, but the more you practice it, the more it becomes a habit that sticks. Is that Starbucks latte worth those extra eight dollars when you can just make it at home? Soon enough, only by asking myself this simple question, I was saving money.

If I wanted fast food while I was out, I thought of my mother's famous line, "*Hay comida en la casa.*" (There's food in the house.)

This was enough for me to not spend unnecessary money. I had a goal in mind and would do anything to achieve it. I started with the end in mind and let that guide my daily actions.

One thing I wish I knew sooner was the importance of financial advisors. As a young woman of color, I never even knew about financial advisors until after college because one reached out to me via LinkedIn who is now my personal financial advisor. When I was growing up, my parents handled all their own finances and never got a proper education on finance. With the help of my financial advisor, I was able to create a debt payoff strategy, establish savings goals, invest in my life insurance, and get on board with my company's 401(k) program. They don't have to cost you any money either! Ask around. You never know who might have someone to refer to you! I currently don't pay to have a financial advisor. That just goes to show you the power of connection.

When pursuing your goals, your *why* has to be stronger than any excuses you'll create for yourself. I dug deeper. Why did I want to pay off my loans? I thought about what came after. I was moving out on my own. I would no longer have to share a room and bed with my mother. I would have the bandwidth to buy the food I wanted. The space I needed to think freely. This was my drive, my motivation.

Funny story. Right after graduating in May 2019, I aspired to move out by October. I'm pretty sure we all know how that turned out. Living at home again with my mother and brother well over a year later, I didn't feel as free as I did before. Sometimes you have to choose your battles. I stuck around at home, and it's been a good decision. We have improved our family relationships, and most of all, I have saved tons of money. If I can leave you with one piece of advice, I suggest living with your parents until you can't take it anymore. Communicate the issues you have with your parents and figure out ground rules. Communication is key wherever you go. Communication is what has allowed me to thrive while living at home. I don't hate the idea of it as I once did after graduation.

Remember, money may not come to you as quickly as you want but be wise with how you choose to spend it. *Get right within* before investing in products to get right on the outside. Before you invest thousands of dollars on skin care, haircuts, hair products, and all other self-care items, make sure you take care of your spirit first. Feed your spirit, and the rest will come. Feed your body nutritious foods. Express gratitude for what already exists in your life. Take care of your mental and physical health before you chase money. When you get right within, people will feel that powerful energy you have. You will attract everything else into your life.

### WHAT I DID TO GET RIGHT WITHIN

Good habits tend to attract more good habits over time. I changed my eating patterns, working out and building confidence from within, which then allowed me to be confident with my finances. I wouldn't feel the need to buy expensive skin care products if I were eating the right foods and working out. I knew that what I needed wasn't on the outside. Instead, everything you need is right inside you. That's not to say that you shouldn't invest on expensive skincare products but always make sure you're right within.

### HOW I SAVED MONEY AND USED MY SKILLS TO MY ADVANTAGE

Getting your fingernails done professionally costs a ton of money. I went on YouTube and learned how to do my own nails with both acrylic and dip powder. Yes, ladies, you can save yourself hundreds, even thousands, of dollars by going on YouTube and learning these skills. I also learned how to do my own box braids after realizing how much time, effort, and money it took for someone else to do it for me. I turned to my best friend, YouTube, and learned. **LinkedIn will be your best friend for work and professionalism. Google will be your best friend for research. YouTube will be your best friend on how to learn new things—from saving money to doing your own hair. Don't downplay your potential skills.** The possibilities are endless.

Here's a powerful thought: How many hours of work did you put in to pay for that product or service? This helped me think deeper about how much I was spending. It may seem simple, but when you realize how society works, equating time to money instead of value to money, you will be better able to manage your finances. The moment I figured out that one cocktail cost two hours of work, I no longer considered it worth it. I could make the same drink at home for much less and save money and time. Let this be your thought process until you get to the point in your life where you can equate value to money—for example, when running a business, having your own course, or booking speaking engagements.

The sooner you save, the more your money grows, and the easier it gets to maintain the habit. You may not be earning much right out of college, and that's okay, but time is on your side. That's important. Putting aside even small amounts regularly now could make the difference between living comfortably as you get older or constantly worrying over your finances. The last thing you want to do is be forty and still stressed over financial decisions you made in your twenties. As of July 2020, while living at home, I put 80 percent of my pay checks toward savings and the rest to my checking account to pay my bills or for any courses or books I wanted to purchase or other basic necessities. I could do this because, living at home, I wasn't paying rent or for groceries or any other expensive necessities.

The 50-30-20 rule is a doable formula. The basic guideline is 50 percent of your income after taxes goes to basic expenses (rent, utilities, groceries). Discretionary spending (vacations, big nights out) is 30 percent. Saving or paying off debt is 20 percent. You can alter these percentages to your liking, but Senator Elizabeth Warren popularized this standard rule.[17]

Even before I had a large income prior to July 2020, I took a sheet of loose-leaf paper, (yes loose-leaf paper, that ancient thing students barely use nowadays) and calculated how much debt I had (student loans, credit card), how much I was making (allowance, side gigs, job), and how much I was spending (food, nights out, bills). This allowed me to clearly visualize where I needed improvement and where I was doing well. I started my money jar and started saving 30 to

---

17    Eric Whiteside, "What Is the 50/20/30 Budget Rule?"

45 percent of what I was making since I had no big expenses. This has allowed me to start paying off loans, clearing my credit card debt, and investing in myself through buying books, courses, or subscriptions that are helping me level up.

One good way to enforce savings is to enroll in your employer's 401(k) plan if they offer that option. A percentage of money comes out of every pay check before taxes, better known as pre-tax. Some employers offer a 401(k) match, which means for every dollar you put in, they match it up to a certain percentage. This is free money. Get as much as you can. Get the most value for working at your job.

Paying off debt doesn't only include savings and making more money. Finance experts at Investopedia discuss two methods to pay off debt. Identify which payoff method would work best for you. That's the start of your plan. Always have a financial plan. First, you can go with the snowball method; here you focus on paying the smallest debts first. The idea behind this method is if you see the smaller debts cleared first, you feel like you can get out of debt altogether. It keeps you motivated to keep going. Second is the avalanche method. Instead of focusing on small balances and building from the bottom up, you prioritize your debts with the highest interest rates. The idea behind this method is to start big and go down from there.[18] Ultimately, debts with the highest interest rates cost the most to keep over time. Whether you're trying to decide to pay off your credit card or your loans first, figure out your rates and create a plan for yourself.

---

18 Ashley Eneriz, "Debt Avalanche vs. Debt Snowball: What's the Difference?"

When figuring out a loan repayment method (for those of you who are blessed with thousands of dollars in loans), make sure that if you make more than the minimum required payment, your overpayments are applied toward your principal balance. If you aren't clear with money lenders, they will put it toward your "future interest," making the debt payoff process much longer than it needs to be. This is how they trick you and why ten-year and twenty-year debt payoff plans exist. Being naïve about money can cost you in the long run.

You are now able to create a debt payoff plan and savings strategy for yourself. Learn from my mistakes. I share this advice with you all because I've lived through it. Right after graduating college, I changed my relationship with money to achieve my goals. Goals to pay off all my student debt, goals to buy a home and move out, and goals to buy whatever I want and not have to worry if I have enough money in my bank account or not. If you tell yourself you're only going to save $1,000, you will only do that. Dream big, and don't lose sight of your goals.

> *Tons of tools are available to help you save money while shopping online. The Honey browser extension automatically searches for coupon codes, applying the codes that allow for the biggest savings at checkout. Websites like CamelCamelCamel track price fluctuations on Amazon and other shopping sites. You can also get email notifications when an item you want falls below a certain price. Rakuten, also known as Ebates, gives cash back options. During one holiday season, I decided to sign up for this and ended up getting money deposited into my checking account.*

**CHAPTER TASK**

Read one book on finance (take your pick) and/or watch at least five videos coaching you on how you can better your finances in your twenties.

Visualize what is possible for your life. Just because you're going through some obstacles now (or you're not currently where you want to be) doesn't mean that will be the case forever.

# CHAPTER 7:

# DO YOUR THING

---

Contrary to popular belief, your major does not define you. That is okay. You are allowed to reinvent yourself after graduation just like I did.

Jason Shen is the co-founder and CEO of Headlight, a performance hiring company, creator of The Talent Playbook, and has been featured in the *New York Times* and the *Atlantic*. In Shen's *TED Talk*, he discusses that the majority of people end up with careers that don't match their major. According to him, over 80 percent of college graduates do not land a job in their "major role."[19] This will take time for them to digest, since most of us come out of college thinking we're going to get a job ideally correlated to our major.

For me, coming out of college, I did not know what I wanted to do. I left college with an open mind about the possibilities. Although I had graduated with a Bachelor of Arts in Latin American and Caribbean area studies, I didn't let this limit

---

19  *TED Residency*, "Jason Shen: Looking for a Job? Highlight Your Ability, Not Your Experience."

my job options. I took a chance and graduated with no plan. No structure or anything really. I knew so many opportunities existed now that I was at home in New York City, opportunities I hadn't previously had in Binghamton. I explored my options through different types of events—panels, one-on-one discussions, and anything in between. Exploring my options seemed like the best thing to do, because in reality, I was lost.

Some of my favorite events I attended during the summer after graduation were put on through:

- Grow with Google. I attended to gain some new skill sets. These workshops covered a range of topics, but some of the ones I enjoyed had to do with building a business and getting it online.
- The Hispanic Federation. These workshop topics ranged from how to write a grant proposal to how to leverage social media for your business.
- General Assembly. They have a wide array of events, but the ones I attended had to do with digital marketing, which I pursued for a little while to gain knowledge of things I should be doing with my brand, Grow with Gera.

I went to events at Salesforce and felt like I was on top of the world—we could legitimately see all of Manhattan from where we were. I didn't even know what Salesforce was while in college, but after being in that room, I learned the impact they had not only in the sales world but in the global world through their community service initiatives, helping out underserved communities across the globe.

I knew I wanted to work with individuals who were giving back to disadvantaged communities. This was one of the top priorities on my job search list. Coming from an underserved community myself, extending a hand to those in need had always been a goal of mine.

## SPEAK YOUR TRUTH

Although I was the youngest in every room I entered, I never limited myself. I didn't let that affect me negatively. I held myself to a higher standard and knew I was meant to be there. Being the youngest in the room allowed me to leverage making connections because people were surprised I was even in these spaces.

Not only was I the youngest, but I came prepared. Everywhere I went, I carried a notepad and pens with me to take notes. Over the past few months, I've learned you never know when an event will pop up, especially living in a big city like New York City. Always be prepared, dress accordingly, and carry a notepad and pen and printed resumes. These became as essential as carrying lip gloss or a phone charger in my bag. I have always been a forgetful person but writing down what was said allowed me to better retain the information and create posts on LinkedIn and videos on Instagram about my experiences at these networking events.

**Always do your research**, and I mean *always*. If I knew I wanted to talk to a specific individual on a panel, I would write down their name, the points they shared, and the things that resonated with me. This gave me a talking point to start with when I decided to approach them. This told them that I was actively listening and taking notes *and* that I cared about what they said. People enjoy hearing about themselves, and when you share this, they resonate more with you, and you can more easily build a bond. Even when you feel alone, the impact of putting yourself out there allows you room to grow.

**Being alone is when you really discover yourself.** Being alone allowed me to explore interests I didn't know I had. For example, I started a blog because I no longer had my girlfriends at arm's reach when I needed to get something off my chest and decided to take up blogging as my escape. Reading also allowed me to continue growing. Reading is so much more fun when you're not forced to do it. I read books instead of just skimming them like I always did as an undergrad. My favorite genres to dive in to are personal development and self-help books. These books have paved the way for my life's transitions.

A lot of people may tell you "adulting sucks," but life is what you make it, so use what you can control to make this one beautiful. Don't let people project their bad life experiences on to you.

You have control over where you work, spend your time, and allocate your energy. Do not let companies take advantage of the "new kid on the block." They will try and underpay you and underestimate you. Know your worth and feel comfortable standing your ground. Things aren't handed out for free in the real world, unfortunately, so if you have information supporting how you've improved yourself like with a business or any company, state those things. **Never undervalue yourself.**

When it comes to money, especially as a first-generation Afro-Latina graduate, I do not play. If you receive an offer, negotiate your salary, check out PayScale to see salary ranges for the position, and do your research. Always go high and never aim low. The sky's the limit.

During this transition period, **you will need constant reassurance that you are worthy and equipped.** I am here to give you that reassurance. Things won't come to fruition overnight, so you need to be prepared. Although your job search requires constant work, you will get the job that you want. You are worthy of being there. You must be patient during this time because not everything will come as quickly as you expect it to. Perhaps you may not get your dream job for three or five years, but everything will occur the way it is supposed to.

Continue working hard, and the blessings will come. Think about this: you spend three to seven years in college working toward your diploma, which you earn through hard work and dedication. Everything else that is good in life comes through the same efforts. In most cases, you don't get married to your first girlfriend or boyfriend; it takes time to find someone genuinely on your level. Obtaining the body of your dreams doesn't come overnight either; it takes time working out, eating healthy, and being mindful. Once you are able to sit comfortably with the reality of hard work, you will start to trust the process and live a more fruitful life. All we have is time. Work with it, not against it. Be patient.

It may feel like adversities are raining down on you for quite some time, but after the rain comes a rainbow and the sun.

Light shines at the end of your journey. Darkness requires light. The first step to success is believing, believing you can achieve whatever you set out to be, no matter how hard. As Aaliyah once said, "If at first you don't succeed, dust yourself off and try again."

**CHAPTER TASK**

I want you to attend one webinar or one networking event. Take notes and reflect on what you gained from this experience and exposure.

# CHAPTER 8:

# HEALTHY HABITS

---

We all possess habits, good or bad. Habits form our daily lives. After college, I realized I had developed some habits that were not going to be beneficial to me in this next stage of life. I could no longer drink the way I used to, take naps all day, stay up all night, and then go on about my day. These things weren't going to suffice anymore. College is like being in your own bubble, in your own world. Now I had to integrate with society, the adult world. What I was doing at nineteen years old was no longer going to contribute to the success I was trying to build. The first step to changing my habits was acknowledging what they were. This helped me better navigate what I had to do to get to the next stage in my life.

Your twenties are a huge developmental period that set you up for the rest of your life, so treat them as such. Meg Jay is a clinical psychologist and author. Her work has appeared on NPR and in the *New York Times*, *Los Angeles Times*, *USA Today*, and *Psychology Today*. Meg is the author of *The Defining Decade: Why Your Twenties Matter—and How to Make the Most of Them Now*. Selected as a "Best Book of 2012" by *Slate* magazine. In Meg Jay's *TED Talk*, "Why 30 is Not the

New 20," she states that the first ten years of a career has an exponential impact on how much money you're going to earn.[20] We know that more than half of Americans are married, living with, or dating their future partner by thirty. Your brain caps off its second and last growth spurt in your twenties as it rewires itself for adulthood.

Essentially, your twenties are more important than people make them seem. Whatever you wish to change about yourself now is the time to change it. Your personality changes more during your twenties than at any other point in your life. Your twenties are a critical period of adult development, defining decades of adulthood. The science behind Jay's talk explains that when you push things off to your thirties, you live with enormous pressure to jump-start a career, to have kids, be financially independent, and more.

"Forget about your identity crisis and get some identity capital," says Jay. Identity capital is doing something that adds value to who you are, an investment in who you might want to be next. Perhaps instead of watching Netflix all day, watch motivational videos on YouTube or *TED Talks*. This is a long-term investment in yourself. All it takes is one phrase, one video, one word to change your outlook on life. I always ask myself this: *Do you want to die with regrets, or do you want to die fulfilled?* That question has helped guide a lot of decisions in my life.

Your twenties are the time to be risk averse. You are essentially remaking your life. You are no longer a student in

---

20  *TED2013.* "Meg Jay: Why 30 Is Not the New 20."

traditional school; you are a student of life now; you are free and capable of doing what you want. If you want to start a business, start it. If you want to work at a company you love but fear you don't have enough experience for, still apply. Go big. Only you know your true potential. When you set limits, you sell yourself short.

I made a lot of lifestyle changes that have aided my success. One of the big decisions I had to make was to stop my heavy drinking. I was a massive drinker in college. We'd have a snow day, and I'd wake up my house with shots. This couldn't be my life anymore. The hangovers were not worth it. My goals outweighed my desire to drink, and now I can say I am headed down the right path. Drinking had led me to put on extra pounds and had messed big time with my mental health. As the wise Simon Cowell once said, "It's a no from me." At this next stage of my life, I wanted to let go of the old and bring in the new.

Throughout my time in college, I gained over fifty pounds, which stemmed from stress and led to bad eating and drinking habits as coping mechanisms. I always felt sluggish and had little energy. I was the nap queen; my friends knew not even to try and open my closed door. I would cook full-blown, five-course meals at 1:00 a.m. after getting home from a long day of classes and meetings.

In this next stage of my life, I made it my duty to be more mindful about what I was putting into my body for my physical and mental well-being. The moment I changed my diet, an active three-year-old seemed to take over my body. I felt more alive; I woke up earlier. I took fewer naps and was more productive throughout my day. You truly learn the power of nutrition after eating terribly for so long. Food is fuel.

All of my growth was made possible because of self-awareness. One of the most important things you can be in life is self-aware. Self-awareness is having a clear perception of your personality, including your strengths and weaknesses, thought patterns, beliefs, values, and emotions. It requires vulnerability with yourself. Self-awareness allows you to understand how people perceive you and also enables you to understand other people. Being self-aware will allow you to have accountability with yourself and with others. Being self-aware will allow you to succeed in life.

Because I was self-aware, I recognized what areas I needed to improve in and what areas I was doing well in, and this helped me form habits that better suited my new lifestyle. I believe everyone should go through this self-evaluation and figure out what you need now and make changes accordingly. The moment I decided to drink less alcohol, get my daily steps in, work out regularly, commit to a meditation session, and go to sleep at a decent hour, things turned around. Creating healthy habits for myself helped me both short term and long term and allowed me to achieve greater professional success and improved my overall state of well-being.

For you to come out of one bad habit, you need to foster a new healthy habit and stay consistent with it. My suggestion would be to write down your current habits, acknowledge some areas you need to work on, and list some things you do well. Do not focus only on the negative! Ultimately, you want to create healthier habits to help you live a better life. Healthy habits have helped my spirit thrive. I feel more aligned and more awake than ever before.

My healthy habits have allowed me to take on a more positive perspective. I became more optimistic, which in turn attracted more optimism in my life.

Matt Cutts shows us how in the span of thirty days, anything is possible. He works for the US Digital Service, a nonpartisan technology agency in the US executive office that improves government services millions of Americans rely upon. In Matt Cutts' *TED Talk*, "Try Something New for 30 Days," he explains that time becomes more memorable when you focus on the progressive changes you are making. "If you want something badly enough, you can do anything for thirty days."[21] This was his motivation. He took a small experiment, thought about something he's always wanted to do, and did it for thirty days. His goals were to take ten thousand steps a day, bike to work, take a picture every day, and write a novel. He subtracted watching television, being on Twitter, and consuming sugar and caffeine. Cutts states that thirty days is just the right amount of time to add a new habit or subtract one. The idea behind these thirty-day challenges is that by making small changes, they become more sustainable.

The thirty-day challenges he partook in helped his self-confidence. He now sets out to do a new challenge every thirty days. It's been years since his *TED Talk*, and he continues this activity. Cutts sees himself as an experimentalist, and

---

21   *TED2011,* "Matt Cutts: Try Something New for 30 Days."

this stemmed from a television show called *30 Days*, more specifically from Morgan Spurlock, its creator. For Cutts, the thrill came from writing an *X* on a calendar after executing his daily tasks. He wanted to keep his streak going, so he wouldn't go to sleep until he completed the tasks.

He doesn't like to plan his goals for the next thirty days too far in advance, so when a new month is about to roll around, a week prior to his new challenge, he analyzes what he wants to do. He asks himself, "What is bothering me? What do I need help with?"

Taking a picture every day for the next thirty days is a great example. Matt did this and said it helped him remember his days more. You can give up television and see how much time you have in your days to get more done. You can go for a walk every day, no matter how long.

When people see other people striving, they want to be that person's friend and follow that person on their journey.

*You regret 100 percent of the things you don't try.*

Listening to his talk inspired me to try something new for thirty days.

I set out to write and publish at least one blog post each day. I loved writing and needed to improve on it, so this was my way of putting myself out there. Although I was nervous, I was still able to get it done. After completing this for thirty days, I felt more articulate in my pieces, accomplished that I completed this goal, and disciplined because I stuck to it. If you want to try it sometime, don't wait until the start of the month. Start now. The days will go by regardless. Make those changes and improve yourself. It's time to level up.

Healthy habits will also allow you to attract more like-minded people, helping you reach your goals faster. Once I started posting more about my daily routine, things that have helped me be a more prosperous individual, I attracted more people to my circle whose goals aligned with mine. This is helpful, because even in moments when you feel discouraged and want to give up, you have people around you to hold you accountable and to remind you of your greatness, and most of all, why you started! When I started documenting my weight loss journey, I didn't want to work out or eat healthy some days, but now I had people watching and depending on me to push through so they could see my results and be motivated themselves. This made me want to keep going because I hated letting other people down.

Perhaps you are not ready to be held accountable or you like to work alone. That's okay. Find what works for you. I tend to forget a lot, so I decided to document my habits. For example, I take daily vitamins; I record in my planner when I consume them. I also enjoy documenting what I accomplish throughout the day. This reminds me even on the days I feel like binge watching Netflix that it's okay to do so. You don't always have to be in beast mode or "perfect" every day. Documenting is an excellent way for anyone to reflect on how far they have come.

Healthy habits are a game changer. They changed my life, and I know that if you want to, they can change your life too. Allow yourself to be vulnerable and become self-aware. What does your body need? What does your spirit need? Start building healthy habits today! Try something new for the next thirty days and tell me how it goes. You've got this!

**CHAPTER TASK**

For the next thirty days, formulate two new habits. Tag me on Instagram @geraldinnoemis or email me at geraldin-noemis@gmail.com so I can root for you and cheer you on. I don't care when in the month you begin. Don't use the "I will do it at the beginning of the next month" excuse. Do it now. Give yourself the chance to start. Try something you've always wanted to do. Whether you get at least fifteen minutes of exercise every day or stay off Instagram for thirty days, you get to choose. Document each day, and at the end of the thirty days, reflect on how it made you feel. Thirty days is 720 hours and 4.286 weeks. You've got this. Don't give up on yourself. Remember to start small. Small changes are sustainable long term.

# CHAPTER 9:

# GRATITUDE

---

"When I graduated, I wish I'd known the research showing that future success doesn't lead to happiness. I sometimes get paralyzed by the fear that happiness exists only if I find the perfect job, degree, or position," said Shawn Achor.

Shawn Achor is an American author and speaker known for his advocacy of positive psychology. He is also the author of *The Happiness Advantage* and founded GoodThink, Inc.[22]

Most of us believe a certain major will allow us to access a certain amount of money and that will make us happy. "In truth, the research is clear: happiness exists down almost any life path as long as you are grateful for the present and develop meaningful relationships. Choose optimism and gratitude now and invest more in others, and happiness will be a lifelong advantage as you pursue your dreams." You have to get right within and be grateful for the abundance you

---

22 Jessica Stillman, "10 *TED* Speakers Offer Their Best Advice to College Grads."

have in your life before expecting you will find happiness in a career or any other sector in your life.

One key thing that has allowed me to look at life and be the happiest I've ever been has been gratitude. *Gratitude* is a word we all constantly hear but may not know. Gratitude is the root of all happiness. Gratefulness has allowed me to take on a new perspective in life. David Steindl-Rast, an American Catholic Benedictine monk, author, and lecturer committed to interfaith dialogue, dealt with the interaction between spirituality and science in his *TED Talk* "Want to Be Happy? Be Grateful." Gratefulness makes us happy.[23] Essentially, he describes gratefulness as something that is freely given to us that holds value. In this sense, every moment is undeserved, and this is why the present is called the present—a freely given gift. If we didn't have this present moment, we wouldn't have the opportunity to experience anything.

Gratefulness is the root of all good. If you're grateful, you're not fearful. If you're not fearful, you're not violent. If you're grateful, you act out of a sense of sufficiency and not a sense of scarcity. My mother has instilled this principle in me from a young age without even realizing it. She always told us to think about how gifted we were. She often reminds me that she and her eleven brothers and sisters ate from one pound of rice and one bag of beans. They took trips walking miles to get water to feed one another. Times were hard, but they were grateful for whatever they could get. Now she has given me and my brother the life she once dreamed of and inspires us to lend a helping hand to others whenever we are able.

---

23   *TEDGlobal 2013*, "David Steindl-Rast: Want to Be Happy? Be Grateful."

Expressing gratitude when you go to bed and when you wake up can set you up for a much more productive and fulfilling day. Gratefulness allows you to see past the little difficulties in life. You can look at the bigger picture. You can be mad that someone stepped on you while in the grocery store or you can be grateful you have access to the grocery store to get the things you need.

I have firsthand experience with this. I have a gratitude journal that I write in every day. Every day I try to write something different I am grateful for. I also unwind from my day in my journal. It allows me to clear my mind and rest peacefully before I go to bed. Self-care.

I express gratitude throughout my day from the moment I open my eyes to the moment I fall asleep. This has allowed me to see my life filled with abundance. I am now attracting more positivity because I look for everything to be grateful for—even the "bad" moments. "Bad" moments can allow you to pivot, find new directions, and learn a lesson. All the "bad" moments and rejections led me to where I am now, and without these experiences, I wouldn't have been able to learn these lessons. If you want to live a happy and fulfilled life, practice gratitude.

We are taught to practice gratitude as early as we are able to walk. What do you do when you see a stop sign? You stop, look, and go. Use the same method with gratitude.

Stop. Don't rush through life because that is how you miss opportunities. We have to build stop signs into our lives. I realized this when my life was flashing by and I was so eager to reach my goals that I wouldn't allow myself time to even think, breathe, and take in what was around me. I was too focused on what I didn't have, and this made me rush.

Now I stop and admire all I have. Open all your senses to the wonderful richness given to us. Enjoy your gifts. Go ahead and open your heart to opportunities you will attract. In the midst of the craziness always going on in the world, I look within and think about how blessed and fortunate I am to stand on my own two feet and have a roof over my head and food on the table. Go and do whatever you want with what life offers you. This is your opportunity to enjoy.

Find balance between being grateful for everything you have while not neglecting what you're dealing with. As humans, we go through stuff that is out of our control sometimes, for example, the loss of a loved one or a job. Seek balance. I had to learn this the hard way while mourning the loss of my cousin and seeing how it hurt my whole family. While I was sad we had lost him, I was still grateful for the moments I had with him and the memories we shared. I was still able to go to my therapist and speak about how I felt about this and keep my head up. I still cry some days just thinking about it, but we have to be grateful for all the little things in life and cherish every moment.

The energy of the universe works in such a way that if you give good, you get good, and vice versa. I've had a prosperous life because I always try and give back, even in the simplest forms. I make it my duty to donate clothes at least once every quarter. I donate food to shelters and to people. I say all of this not to brag but to share that when you do things out of the kindness of your heart, they will come back tenfold. I always went home feeling happy about what I did because, as stated earlier, one of my lifelong goals is to eradicate homelessness forever.

I feel everyone should have a roof over their head and food to eat, and this is why I do small acts of kindness. Every time I do a good deed, something good happens for me shortly after. I can't explain why, but that's how the universe works. My parents are the same way, and although they've faced hardships in their lives, they have become comfortable and are fulfilled with where they have gotten in life. Although they don't have the most money in the world, they could have a dollar in their pocket and they would still give it to someone in need because acting from a place of abundance, even if you don't have it all, is the cornerstone of their lives.

**Just because something isn't your reality doesn't mean it isn't someone else's. We can be grateful for and happy about so many things in this life.** The future of the world will be a network, not a pyramid. Grateful people are joyful people. Be grateful. You're blessed even in your worst moments.

**CHAPTER TASK**

Every day for the next seven days, write three things you're grateful for. At the end of the week, look back at what you have written and assess how this makes you feel. Build a habit of practicing gratefulness in your everyday life. Who knows what it could do?

# CHAPTER 10:

# EXPERIENCES

———

Your life is cultivated from your experiences. One of the best things I did while in college was join clubs. I had to find my community while attending a predominantly white institution. These clubs shaped my life and molded me to be the leader I am today.

**ADVICE TO UNDERGRADUATES**
Joining clubs allows you to build your professional skills because now you have to work with people with different attitudes and different backgrounds.

You learn active listening skills, how to collaborate with groups, and how to lead, and you engage in thoughtful conversation. Many of us undersell our experiences in these clubs because they aren't big corporations, but clubs lay the foundation for your professional life. All the leadership skills I acquired in college were through hosting sorority events. I lacked work ethic prior to this experience, but afterward I could lead a room all by myself and command attention.

My journey has been a long one. I used to be scared of leading discussions in front of big groups because I doubted my ability to formulate my thoughts. I didn't feel I knew enough to share my ideas. I always felt I couldn't keep up with everyone else. However, I was pushed past my comfort zone and found I *could* lead these events when I joined my sorority.

This forced me into my early days in leadership and helped me get out of my head and in front of people. I had one-on-ones and work meetings and spoke up because I no longer felt my voice didn't matter.

I used to be so scared of what people would think about me, but that changed once I realized I could speak for voiceless people. I speak not to benefit myself but to help guide those around me. Don't ever undervalue your experiences; they are what made you who you are today.

By joining clubs, you surround yourself with people who want to do similar things and have the same interests. In this day and age, you can make a career out of anything. I've seen people quit jobs they hate as lawyers to become comedians in local bars because they love it. I've seen people lose it all and find themselves in that moment of loss because they look within and surround themselves with like-minded people. If you're trying to become a doctor, join a club for aspiring doctors. Hang around medical professionals, don't hang around people who aren't going where you're trying to go because they will only hold you back. The power of connections and meeting people is key.

Always follow your gut. Even if you have the slightest interest in something, try it and see what happens. I remember going to glee club auditions even though none of my friends were interested in it. I knew it might spark my interest because singing was a passion of mine. Although I didn't get in, that didn't stop me from trying something new. I continued to explore new clubs to surround myself with the right communities.

You will never know the outcome unless you try. Do not limit yourself to what you can't do. Instead, take advantage of all opportunities. Try it all out because after graduation, a lot of people leave confused, unsure about what they want. Take all those career life quizzes and emotional intelligence quizzes. Find out more about yourself. **Tap inward for what you're searching for outward.** If you want to be successful, search for successful people. What are they doing? What interests do they have? What clubs or organizations are they a part of?

If you need help creating a routine, ask for advice from those successful people. What is their background? How do they start their mornings?

Based on what I've learned and done within my own life, I can share five tips that will help mold your success:

1. **Wake up early.** Get at least eight hours of sleep and create a routine for yourself. This isn't college anymore. You don't have to stay on campus 'til 1:00 a.m. for meetings or stay up 'til 3:00 a.m. for homework or for an exam you had all month to study for. Now you run on your own

time. Make it your duty to fall asleep earlier so you can wake up earlier and get more done with your day. I didn't believe early rising mattered that much until I tried it myself and saw my improved productivity. If you stay focused for six months, you can put yourself five years ahead. Now is your time to do it. Get adequate sleep, wake up early, and focus on you.

2. **Focus on consistency, not instant gratification.** I had to learn this the hard way. I have rushed so many things in life. I haven't enjoyed the full experience because I was seeking instant gratification. My weight loss journey and the development of my professional skills has taught me that consistency helps you overcome. Consistently eating the right foods, working out, and honing the new skills you learn will, over time, truly prove to be superior.

3. **Use your imagination.** Allow yourself to be creative. The same way I used to brainstorm ideas for meetings to host and event topics, you can use your creativity to keep you young. I like to use my imagination during my own personal projects and while working. Work then becomes less tedious and more enjoyable.

4. **Seek knowledge.** Knowledge is power. I wish I would've learned this sooner, maybe then I would've read more business books while in undergrad. Seek knowledge, whether it be through books, podcasts, videos, or courses. Wherever you find it, look to learn at least one new thing every day. I've studied and learned a lot about topics that interest me, and I am now able to monetize this knowledge in some ways and share it with uninformed communities too.

5. **Get rid of distractions.** If it doesn't serve your higher good, don't let it take up too much space in your life.

The fewer distractions you have, the more focused you are and the more you're able to get ahead and thus find balance in your life.

**BE REAL**

Authenticity has always helped me succeed in my positions, whether as an undergraduate leader or an employee at a company.

Don't let negativity dim your light in any room. Let your realness shine. With anything you do in life, people will easily disregard you if they don't find you believable or relatable. You can hear authenticity in your voice, see it through a screen, and read it on your face. Be that person. Most people just tell employers what they want to hear. Instead, be you. If they don't like you for you, then you weren't meant to be there in the first place, and a better opportunity will come along. Being the real you will get you real friends, so put yourself out there to meet diverse individuals.

Your experiences are unique to you. Allow them to tell your story and cultivate richer life experiences. Your experiences hold tremendous value and can help you navigate your life's GPS to reach your destination. Good or bad, your experiences make you the bright, charismatic, and unique individual you are today.

**CHAPTER TASK**

Journal for a week as an act of self-care. Allow your most vulnerable self to come out on paper or via your digital device. See how this makes you feel. If you like it, make it a habit.

Benefits of journaling: Journaling helps you improve your mood, allowing you to prioritize problems, fears, and concerns in order to properly address them. Track any day-to-day symptoms so you can recognize triggers and learn ways to better control them. Journaling provides an opportunity for positive self-talk and enables you to identify negative thoughts.[24]

24  *Health Encyclopedia*, s.v. "journaling for mental health (*n.*)," accessed August 2020.

# CHAPTER 11:

# THE PRESENT

---

Throughout this book, I've explained what I did after graduating college and what led to my success. As we come to the end, I will share a secret with you.

I'm going to show you what I do now and how I continue to pave my way for success not only in my life but in others' lives too. I am only as good as those around me, am I right?

First and foremost, graduating from college allows you to take on a new persona. It allows you to recreate who you are. I chose to change because I was headed down an unhealthy route. This life fostered depression instead of admiration and enjoyment of all life had to offer.

After graduation, I acknowledged my true worth. When you grasp your value, your worth—which is deeper than the surface-level things like the way you physically look—when you see what you have to offer on the inside, your good heart, and your honest intentions, you will realize fear shouldn't dictate your life. Rejection shouldn't control you.

To overcome fear of rejection, first tap into your feelings. What is making you feel a certain way? Rejection can also involve other uncomfortable emotions such as embarrassment. No one else can tell you how to feel. Before addressing your emotions around rejection, acknowledge them. Trying to prove to yourself that you don't care isn't helping anyone, and you are only furthering the hurt. After acknowledging those emotions, look for an opportunity to learn from them. Rejection can provide opportunities of self-growth and self-discovery.

After countless rejections, my first job out of college was working at a restaurant. Although it wasn't what I expected, I still was grateful for the experience. But my first real corporate job out of college was working as a sales development representative for Insider Intelligence.

I got hired in July 2020. A few weeks prior, I was having a full-blown meltdown. I spoke to my father, crying, asking him when my time would finally come? I was jobless, funds were extremely low, and I felt purposeless. My content seemed to not be having an impact. It hurt because I put a lot of time into creating my content (other content creators and creatives know the feeling). It felt like my book was never going to be done. My world was crashing down before my eyes.

Things literally turned around right when I clung to my last string of hope. They say the universe works in mysterious ways, and that's exactly what happened. I got word that I was hired at the end of June.

I share my story because I don't want you to feel discouraged if you see those around you prospering while you wait for an opportunity. Sometimes you don't get the job you want because it's not the one you need. That job won't promote your growth or teach you lessons. The job you want isn't always the one that's best for you, and that's the cold, hard truth. The same thing can be said for opportunities.

Speaking from my corporate experience, I strongly suggest you create a schedule that works specifically for you! I tried to mimic a lot of successful people's daily routines, but it didn't work for me. I learned to use those YouTubers as inspiration for my daily structure.

I start my mornings early. On some days, I do a full-blown workout, and some days I stretch. On others, I meditate. Whatever I choose to do, it helps me get a positive, healthy start. Also, sleep is important! You're no longer in college. You can't run on four hours of sleep (or zero hours of sleep, as I know most of us did while in undergrad). You will feel burnt out, and you will not function! Coffee will not fix you. You need adequate sleep.

Talk to and act toward yourself the same way you do with your friends when they are going through something. Take care of yourself. Give yourself different tips on self-care, and then *do* them. In addition, I love starting my days with tea, and a gallon of water (reusable, of course, to save the environment), and fruits. I've never really been a big breakfast person, but it really does affect how your day turns out. Starting off with breakfast allows me to have my meals earlier, which in turn allows me more time to burn the calories throughout the day. I also made a rule for myself (you can try it too) to have at least one fruit and one veggie every day. Starting my day with fruits allows me to hit one of my goals early and already feel accomplished.

I truly believe your body is a temple, and you have to take care of it accordingly. I decided I no longer wanted to struggle when climbing stairs or carrying groceries every time my mother and I went grocery shopping. We young people don't put enough emphasis on health.

A few months prior to ending college, my doctor told me I was at high risk of getting diabetes. So, I decided to change my eating habits. They did change for a short time. But then I went back to eating crappy food. Just like going back to that messed-up ex you swore you wouldn't return to, that was my relationship with bad foods.

The summer after graduation, I knew I had to make a change. It hasn't been easy, but I started seeing changes in my energy levels once I started eating better. Feed your body what it needs. We all have aspirations to be successful with our lives, so give your body and spirit what they need to get there.

Something I've put great emphasis on since graduating is expressing gratitude. I went twenty-one years without expressing much gratitude for what life had given me. We are given every little thing—waking up in the morning, having water to drink and food to eat, and functioning legs to get you places. Everything is a gift, and we should see it as such. The moment I started looking at every moment as a present, a world of abundance opened up. I look at my goals with a clearer vision now, knowing that everything I want is attainable. Don't let anyone tell you that you can't do something because you can! I am living proof that if you work toward improving yourself 1 percent every day, you will get to where you want to go.

Reframing your mindset to see fear as a chance for growth can make it easier to try what you want and decrease the pain if you fail.

Try telling yourself, "This may not work out, but if it doesn't, I'll have a meaningful experience and know more than I did."

In every opportunity lies a chance to learn a lesson you may not have previously known before. Rejection can be especially scary when you look too deep into it. However, rejection is often as simple as the needs of two parties not matching up. Building self-confidence and self-worth can help you remember you're entirely worthy of everything you want, leading you to feel less afraid of continuing your search for your desires.

Identifying what's really behind your fear can help you address that specific worry. Perhaps you're afraid of romantic rejection because you don't want to feel lonely. Coming to this realization can help you prioritize and develop strong friendships, too, which can help insulate you against loneliness. On the other hand, you may worry about being rejected by potential employers because you feel financially insecure and don't have a plan B. Alleviate this stress by outlining a few possible strategies in case you don't find the job as quickly as you would like. If you're not able to put yourself out there, you won't experience rejection, and you probably won't reach your goals either. Going after what you want increases your chances of achieving success. Create a list of your fears and try to tackle them one by one; if you deal with anxiety, this also can help you conquer that.

Rejecting negative self-talk is also key through this process. Our brains default to be negative. If you continue to put the blame on yourself regardless of actual fault, you will continue to fuel your fear of rejection. Challenge your negative self-talk and replace it with positive self-talk. When you encourage and support yourself, you are more likely to believe in your own potential to achieve your goals. Rejection fears can have a lifelong effect on you; if you constantly struggle with this, seek professional help. You have nothing to be ashamed of. Many people live with this fear day in and day out. Ultimately, I want you to cultivate the life you desire, free of fear.

Don't ever ask for permission to pursue your goals. Show up and do it. Don't question your capabilities. As recent graduates and people unsure of their life trajectory, we tend to do that a lot. We second-guess ourselves, and that stems from fear. To overcome this, we must let that fear go.

One final thing I want to leave you with is the power of consciousness. As stated in previous chapters, I enjoy using affirmations and listening to specific music while I do activities because it helps to tap into my subconscious mind. We only use 5 percent of our conscious mind on an everyday basis. The other 95 percent is untapped potential we like to call the subconscious. I highly suggest you do things such as prayer, affirmation, meditation and listening to music with positive subliminal messages. Over a period of time, you will start seeing changes. We are capable of doing so much when we tap into our subconscious minds. Tapping into my subconscious has allowed me to be more at peace and worry less because I know ultimately everything is going to be okay. It has reduced my anxiety, allowed me to not set limits on myself, and enabled me to attract like-minded people into my life. Start by doing at least one thing every day for your subconscious, whether it be meditating for five minutes or putting on background music with positive subliminal messages while you study or work. I promise you, the benefits you will see are life changing.

Now you may be thinking, "Wow, that's it?"

Don't worry that's not everything.

I have saved perhaps the best for last.

I pride myself on giving advice and helping those around me. I decided to ask a few folks that are close to me what they wish they knew during undergrad to prepare themselves for life after college.

Here's what they had to say:

*"Besides the fact that networking really is everything, I wish I knew about different career paths that weren't the traditional ones we're taught about—doctors, lawyers, and teachers. College is the time to explore all your opportunities without the fear of failure, so take advantage of any internship, externship, volunteer, and shadowing experiences that allow you to get*

insight into different industries that you are (or even think you may be) interested in. Get as much experience and knowledge as you can while you're an undergrad!"

—STEFANIE R.

"As an undergraduate student, I came in completely blind, thinking I could do anything I put my mind to. I thought I was going to college for one specific reason and came out doing something on the opposite end of my spectrum. I was not prepared mentally or emotionally for the amount of stress that came with the classes I needed to take. I was told I needed to take most of my classes at once to 'finish on time,' but really, I had all the time in the world. I felt ambushed by the number of things I had to do. In reality, I could have made my own choices and continued the career path I wanted to take. Ultimately, I had to take a step back and realize college has no real rush. You work at your own pace. As a graduate student, I have come to learn everyone is built differently in all aspects of health, and we need to be okay with the idea of taking ten steps back if needed. During my undergrad career, I wish I was taught that everyone works at their own pace and life after college doesn't require that we hurry. Of course, look for the bigger picture, but do not rush, for our creative minds need more time than we think! Give yourself some time to read the situation and learn from it."

—CINDY R.

"'There is somebody for everyone in college.' That saying is true. So many different types of people colliding mean the only way to not make friends is if you actively avoid it. Herein lies the bittersweet truth. People naturally gravitate toward people that relate to the same experiences, and that's exactly what I did. In college, I spent so much time around people that look like me and had the same ideals as I had that I missed an opportunity to broaden my understanding of different people and different worldly perspectives. Your network is your net worth, and if I could speak to the younger version of myself, I would encourage her to cultivate relationships with different people. The real world is difficult and having a large network can ease that burden because you never know who could change your life for the better."

—PEACE O.

"Learn people. And then learn to love people. Everything we do on Earth is about people, so understanding how to build relationships with, understand, collaborate with, and help others is key for success. If you truly value people, you'll be curious to learn what makes people tick (starting with yourself!). Also, find projects to work on that solve problems you're interested in, bring you around people you enjoy being with, and also bring out the best in you. These projects will help you build transferable skills you can take with you to any job opportunity."

—DANIEL A.

*"I wish I knew the other routes one can take to become an educator. I was so proud to major in childhood education alongside many smart and driven individuals who taught me so much, but most went on to teach in rural or suburban schools where the curriculum doesn't set up students for the success I want. Students should think deeply about the historical texts they read and raise questions about them, creating a culture of critical thinkers who aren't afraid to be wrong or to speak against what's written in history books. I know I listened and believed in that jargon reiterated throughout my entire public education. Never did I ask. I just listened and consumed that information. I didn't seek to learn more or question. Perhaps that is partly my fault, but I don't wish that upon my students. I want them to hold themselves responsible for everything they come across in literature and to ask themselves, 'From whose perspective was this written? What about those groups of people and their voice? What were other people going through during this time period on the other side of the world?' And more. I wish I knew there are many more paths one can take to get where they want or need."*

—SUFIA H.

Unfortunately, all good things have to end at some point. I hope you learned a wealth of information through the experiences and information I have shared in this book. I hope you all follow your passions and give yourself time to grow and to truly manifest. I hope you are kind to yourself and allow yourself to fail, fail forward, fail fast. I hope you fall in love with yourself in the process of self-discovery. I wish you nothing but the best. Know that you always have a friend in me.

**CHAPTER TASK**

Your last task for this chapter is to do one thing that scares you, and I mean really scares you, whether it be going to a networking event, direct messaging someone, shooting your shot with your potential soulmate. Just do it. I want us to release fear and channel possibilities.

With love,

Geraldin

# APPENDIX

---

**INTRODUCTION**

Jacimovic, Darko. "College Graduates Unemployment Rate in the US." What to Become. August 11, 2020.

Kelly, Jack. "Recent College Graduates Have the Highest Unemployment Rate in Decades—Here's Why Universities Are to Blame." *Forbes*. November 14, 2019.

**CHAPTER 1**

Half, Robert. "Millennials: Workplace Rebels or Misunderstood Talents?" RobertHalf.com. Published August 27, 2017.

Kiyosaki, Robert, and Kim Kiyosaki. *The Business of the 21st Century*. Bhopal, India: Manjul Publishing House, 2012.

Schrieberg, Ethan. "The 9-to-5 Workday Is So Last Century." HRTechnologist. Published October 15, 2018.

Swain, Ann. "Flexible Working Increase Five-Fold." HRD Online. September 15, 2019. Accessed August 11, 2020. https://www.thehrdirector.com/business-news/flexible-agile-working/flexible-working-increase-five-fold4072019.

## CHAPTER 2

Armstrong, Victor. "Stigma Regarding Mental Illness among People of Color." National Council for Behavioral Health. July 8, 2019.

David, Eden. "Rising Suicide Rates at College Campuses Prompt Concerns over Mental Health Care." ABC News. October 9, 2019.

"Latinx/Hispanic Communities and Mental Health." Mental Health America. Last modified 2019.

"Mental Health by the Numbers." NAMI: National Alliance on Mental Illness. Last updated September 2019.

Watkins, Andrea. "Benefits of Deep Breathing." *Urban Balance* (blog). 2019.


## CHAPTER 3

Beal, Mark. *Decoding Gen Z: 101 Lessons Generation Z Will Teach Corporate America, Marketers & Media*. New Jersey: Mark Beal Media, LLC, 2018.

Holloway, Anthony. "My 21-Day Job Offer Story." *Medium* (blog). Medium. April 15, 2019.


## CHAPTER 4

Kuchar, Kristen. "Student Loans 101: Vocabulary." The Simple Dollar. February 20, 2020.

Wood, Sarah. "New Survey Finds College Students Lack Financial Literacy." Diverse Issues in Higher Education. July 15, 2019.


## CHAPTER 5

Wood, Sarah. "New Survey Finds College Students Lack Financial Literacy." Diverse Issues in Higher Education. July 15, 2019.


## CHAPTER 6

Eneriz, Ashley. "Debt Avalanche vs. Debt Snowball: What's the Difference?" Investopedia. Updated May 20, 2020.

Whiteside, Eric. "What Is the 50/20/30 Budget Rule?" Investopedia. Updated August 4, 2020.

## CHAPTER 7

*TED Residency.* "Jason Shen: Looking for a Job? Highlight Your Ability, Not Your Experience." Streamed live November 2017. Video, 6:22.

## CHAPTER 8

*TED2011.* "Matt Cutts: Try Something New for 30 Days." Streamed live March 2011. Video, 3:12.

*TED2013.* "Meg Jay: Why 30 is Not the New 20." Streamed live February 2013. Video, 14:37.

## CHAPTER 9

Stillman, Jessica. "10 TED Speakers Offer Their Best Advice to College Grads." Inc.com. Updated May 24, 2018.

*TEDGlobal 2013.* "David Steindl-Rast: Want to Be Happy? Be Grateful." Streamed live June 2013. Video, 14:18.

## CHAPTER 10

*Health Encyclopedia.* Online ed. s.v. "Journaling for Mental Health." Rochester: University of Rochester Medical Center, 2020.

## CHAPTER 11

N/A

# ACKNOWLEDGMENTS

Joel Reyes

Cassie Spencer

Aimme Perez

Heman Armstrong

Lucy Basta

Hilary Hernandez

Gipsy Fermin

Amanda Fernandez

Jose Rivera

Thalia Flores

Dayshane Adorno

Genesis Castro

Renee Martinez

Travis Allen

Thalia Sanchez

Eileen Figueroa

Sufia Hasnat

Jocelyn Cortes

Marlon Pimentel

Eric Koester

Justin Ware

Erin Cody

Ashley Gonzalez Melo

Diku Lima

Michelle Martinez

Joyce Soto

Feliz Aurora Gonzales

Danielle Gutkovich

Michelle Battle

Nikki Merkerson

Oyin Adewale

Nathalie Guerrero

Dalila Frias

Ivan Mendoza

Hamley Volquez

Jae Won Chung

Alex Balili

Kaitlynn Liriano

Michelle Acevedo

Christian Vargas

Luisa Toribio

DeQuentin Overton

Daniela Tlaseca
Maryann Hrichak
Junior Cabrera
Deja Parham
Anastasia Figuera
Julio Reyes
Johanna Figari
Manuel Cabrera
Luis Gonzalez
Yorlenny Medina
Rebeca Mora
Sheydji Rivera
Cristina Cruceta
Johanna Hernandez
Ruddy Ronqullo
Lanique Dawson
Darlenne Goris
Megan Saldanha
Vickie Lin
Sarah Samson
Tina Ouedraogo
Karima Legette
Matthew Franceschini
Ashley Gomez
Jennifer Feliz
Yuri Lee
Avery Nasir
Abdukhalil Khalil
Isaiah Smith
Joleyene Herrera
Alexa Javier
Luis Espinal

Devaunte Collingwood
Osariemen Aiyevbomwan
Shaziya Riya
Yeiny Moreno
Jomarys Solano
Dasia Jones
Daniela Morel
Elizabeth Herrera
Melissa Bornico
Sujayliz Alfred
Liliana Espinal
Taylor Alvarez
Chantel Ayuso
Annie Johansen
Jordan Pedroza
Christina Cerio
Nicole Kumar
Beibei Lubin
Maiya Gonzalez
Ella Wortman
Justin Lazaar
Kristen Crawford
Saul Thelusma
Brianna Infante
Sabrina Cabrera
Andra Espinal
Ashly Cortes
Ampofo Mensah Jr.
Ricardo Martinez
Jalaal Shah-Taylor
Courtney Edwards
Maryam Durosinmi

Geovanni Constanza

Chelsea Cabrera

Ashley Taveras

Zeinah Issah

Ammy Salinas

Minul Asgar

Justine Garcia

Emma Shen

Julia Milewski

Sarah Curtis

Marleen Moise

Deepa Mistry

Brandon Diaz

Karl Ravilus

Tequan Bowie

Joanna Lojo

Connie Torres

Thalia Sanchez

Maria Fajardo

Peace Omoregie

Romarly Valentin

Jasmine Boothe

Jennifer Levy

Benice Boamah

Nahi Ajaka

Dessiree Infante

Ana Q. Reyes

Jesse Donkor

Geancarlo Jordan

Brandon Walker

Sabrina Peralta

Christine Caldero

Gabrielle Ospina

Mario Cabral

Catherine Morales

Erika Aguilera

Hector Almonte

Melissa Rodriguez

Luisanny Molina

Amy Ciriaco

Alexander Boston

Jenny Reyes

Gina Perez

Arryana Olavarria

Aminata Jaiteh

Aylin Gonzalez

Brezhe Brooks

Destiny Ware

Arlene Salazar

Cristhy Azcona

Ikea Carlos

Natasha Jimenez

Jahmal Ojeda

Nafisa Khan

Tracy Wilkins-Dickerson

Catherine Del Monte

Jennifer Santamaria

Jerry Toussaint

Dionne Fraser

Dolores Acosta

Leah Schechter

Samantha Sanchez

Courtney Mitchell

Angel Ramirez

Fatoumata Kane
Angel Avila
Anibel Vargas
Miriam Gallegos
Allen Frimpong
Felix Serrano
Kianna Williams
Lauren Osoria
Chris Mazile
Adeenah Ahmed
Ashley Wells
Lucy Basta

CPSIA information can be obtained
at www.ICGtesting.com
Printed in the USA
LVHW052338111220
673982LV00012B/14